DROPBUX
MADE EASY

Syncing Your Work to the Cloud

By James Bernstein

Bernstein, James
Dropbox Made Easy
Part of the Productivity Apps Made Easy series

For more information on reproducing sections of this book or sales of this book,
go to **www.madeeasybookseries.com**

Contents

Introduction

With everything being done online these days, it seems as though you need to know how to master a multitude of technologies just to get your work done. We are expected to know how to use email, texting, social media, cloud based office productivity services, smartphone apps and so on.

Not too long ago (depending on who you ask), when we wanted to share files and collaborate with our peers, we would have to send files back and forth via email and hope that we were working on the latest version of the file. Doing this would also get complicated when we had many people we were working with on a project at the same time.

Another option was to use what is known as an FTP (File Transfer Protocol) server to store and share files. But this takes some technical skills to set up, and you also need your own server to store these files on. These are still in use today by businesses but are not practical for the home or small business user.

Fortunately, today we have many options as to where we can store and share our files and it seems like we are almost getting pressured into using these services. For example, when you get a new computer running Microsoft Windows, it will try and force you to use their online storage platform called OneDrive. And if you have a Google\Gmail account, you automatically get access to their Google Drive service whether you want it or not!

The goal of this book is to get you signed up with Dropbox and comfortable with the interface when it comes to uploading and downloading files and folders. I will also be going over how to share and collaborate with other Dropbox and non Dropbox users.

Once you understand the main concept of how Dropbox and other cloud storage services work, it will make the experience that much easier and also prepare you to use other online storage services at the same time since not everyone uses Dropbox for their cloud storage needs. So on that note, let's head to the cloud!

Chapter 1 – Cloud Storage Overview

Before showing you how to use Dropbox, I would like to spend a little time going over what exactly it is and what you will expect to see when you first start using it. I will be working with the free account but will also be going over some features of the business account so you can see what you get when you break out your wallet!

What is Cloud Storage?

In order to get an understanding of what exactly Dropbox does, you should first have an idea of the concept of cloud storage. You are probably used to storing your files and folders on your hard drive and maybe use a removable USB hard drive or flash drive to back up your files or transfer them between locations.

Doing things this way is fine for many people but if you are going to be sharing your files with others or want a way to backup important files offsite, then using cloud storage might be the solution you need.

The term cloud storage refers to storing your files on servers that are located at other locations around the country, or even around the world. Then when you access your files and folders, you do so via a web browser or client software over the internet. This allows you to work on your files remotely or download them to your local computer and then sync them back with the server when you save them again.

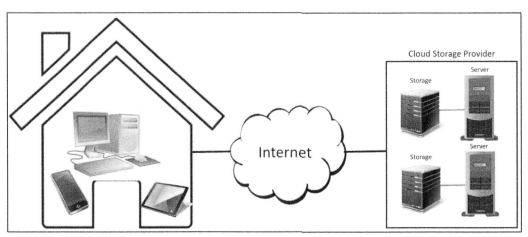

Figure1.1

Types of Cloud Storage
There are four main types of cloud storage typically in use today. I will be focusing on just one of them, but I wanted to go over the others, so you have an idea of what is available out there.

- **Personal Cloud Storage** – This is what we will be focusing on for the most part and is mainly used to store a user's personal data online, allowing them to access it from anywhere that they have an Internet connection and a device capable of accessing their data. This can be done via a desktop computer, laptop, smartphone, or tablet, and all you need to do is sign into your account and you are off and running.

- **Public Cloud Storage** – This is used when a company doesn't have its own cloud storage resources and all of the infrastructure for the storage is managed off-site by another company which also takes care of all aspects of the cloud storage, including making sure it's available all the time and also backed up. Public Cloud Storage providers will store data from many customers all at the same location.

- **Private Cloud Storage** — If a company wants to utilize cloud storage and have it located within their own datacenter but still be managed by a third party, then they can take the private route. This is common when the data is private or confidential and the company needs to know where it is at all times.

- **Hybrid Cloud Storage** — Hybrid Cloud Storage is a combination of Public and Private Cloud Storage where a company will have its critical data stored at its own location while having less important data be stored at the cloud provider's location.

Benefits of Cloud Storage
Not all cloud storage is the same, so the benefits will vary based on the type you choose. Since we are only dealing with the personal type, that is what I will be focusing on going forward.

I have many clients that I do work for, and one thing that is very common between a lot of them is the lack of backups. (That is until I force them to start doing them!) If you are like most people, then you have many (or even too many) pictures on your computer as well as music and documents that you would be very upset about losing. If you don't do a backup, then you risk a disaster if your hard drive fails or at least the potential to spend a lot of money on a data recovery service.

Even if you do backup your data at home or at the office, there's a chance of losing it in situations involving such things as fires or floods. In fact, many companies who do their own local backups will have a service that comes by and takes their backups to a secure location offsite to ensure that they will always be safe.

For us home users having a personal backup assistant is not an option, so we are on our own to make sure we have our data securely backed up. This is where having a cloud storage account can come in handy. If you copy your important files to a location in the cloud, then they are safe there in case something happens to your computer or the location of where your computer is stored. In a worst-case scenario you can get your computer back up and running and then restore your files from your cloud backup right to your computer.

Another benefit of cloud storage is having your data available all the time, no matter where you are. Let's say you are out of town on vacation and brought your laptop or tablet with you and need to get a copy of your resume to apply for a job you want to get in on right away. If you have your data in the cloud, all you would have to do is log on to your account, download your resume, and send it off. Many times there are options to create a link right to a specific file that you can email to someone, but I will get into that later.

Another way to use cloud storage to your benefit is when you are collaborating with other people on a team project and need to share information. Depending on what cloud provider you go with, you will usually have the option to share files and folders with other people and assign levels of permissions to those people so nobody can get away with doing something they shouldn't be doing to your files, plus it will usually show the last person who made a change to a file with the date and time.

We are all familiar with computer viruses and spyware and how they can ruin our day when they infect our computers. Some of them can even encrypt your files make them inaccessible to you forever. Plus, there's always the chance of you sending an infected file to someone else and infecting their computer. If you have a backup of your files in the cloud, then they will be safe from getting infected (assuming you have not uploaded the infected files to your cloud location).

Disadvantages of Cloud Storage
Many companies use cloud-based storage and applications to save money because they don't need to buy the hardware to support them and hire IT people to maintain them. The main downside is that if you lose your Internet connection

then you lose access to your storage and programs, but for big corporations, it's rare that they have much or any downtime.

For us home users, we have the same types of choices, but on a smaller scale. Here are some of the *disadvantages* of cloud storage:

- **Dependency on the Internet** – Since you need Internet access to get to your files in the cloud, you will have to rely on your Internet service to be up. If you lose your Internet connection, then you won't be able to access your files unless you downloaded a copy to your computer. Home users tend to not have the same reliability when it comes to their Internet connection as big companies do. That's most likely because these corporate accounts cost much more money.

- **Trusting a third party with your data** – Since you don't know *exactly* where your files are being stored and who *really* has access to them, you will have to put some trust in your cloud provider. For all you know, your files may be sitting somewhere in another country with who knows who looking at them.

- **Cost** – Many cloud storage providers will allow you to have a small amount of storage space for free with the plan of enticing you to buy more space once you fill up the free space they've provided. This can get costly if you have a lot of data since the free accounts will only hold so much.

- **Performance** – If you have a slow Internet connection or have huge files, then you will need to wait for your files to download or upload. Plus, if you are working on your smartphone using your cellular connection, it might be even slower.

For the most part, you have nothing to lose in trying out a free cloud storage provider like Dropbox to see if it is something you would like to use on a regular basis. Then you can determine if the cost is worth the advantages you get from keeping your data in the cloud, or if you don't feel comfortable using this type of service.

Free vs. Paid Plans

I mentioned before how most of these personal cloud storage providers will offer you an opportunity to use their service for free with a limited amount of storage space. The main reason they do this is so you will start using the service and get to the point where you run out of space for your free account and then are forced to start paying for the service to get more space for your files. This is understandable because all these companies need to make money somehow or else they wouldn't be in business.

Usually with free accounts, you don't get the same level of support as you would when paying for the service. If you are not too computer savvy, then it will probably benefit you to have that extra level of support in case things go wrong. There is nothing worse than needing an important file that you don't have on your device and not being able to get it from your cloud storage!

Often there are other advantages to having a paid account besides better customer service. For example, the pay-for version might let you share your storage with family and friends, recover deleted files, or even restore older versions of files in case you made a change you want to reverse.

The biggest benefit to having a paid account is the increase in storage space. Most of the time you will have the choice of different levels of storage space at different levels of pricing, and if you choose one level and find out you need more space, then you can simply upgrade your plan without having to re-upload all of your files.

So, when it comes to choosing your cloud storage provider, make sure to check out all the additional features you get if you decide you might go with a plan that will cost you money so you know exactly what extras you will be getting for your dollar. If you only have a small amount of data and don't plan on having too much or any growth, then you should be just fine with a free plan.

Web Based vs. Desktop Client
When it comes to cloud storage one of the most important things to consider is the ease of access to your files. If you have to deal with some clunky, hard to manage interface, then you might find yourself not even wanting to use the service. Of course, just like with anything else new, you will need to get used to accessing your files this way.

Most cloud storage services give you the option to access your files via a web browser or by using a program or app that you install on your computer or smartphone\tablet. For the most part, you can use your favorite web browser and things should be fine, but if you notice that something doesn't seem to work the way it should or seems a little buggy, then you might want to try a different web browser. Fortunately, you can install as many browsers as you like on your computer or smartphone such as Google Chrome and Mozilla Firefox, or use the built in browsers such as Microsoft Edge and Apple Safari, depending on the operating system used by your device.

Many times the program or app for the cloud storage service will work better and be faster than the web browser method because it's designed to work with the storage service. Sometimes it will even have more features than the browser method, so it's a good idea to try out any app that might be available.

On the other hand, any device that can access the Internet should have a built-in web browser that you can use rather than having to install an app on each one of your devices. (By the way, when I say "devices" I am referring to things like computers, laptops, smartphones, and tablets.) You might also run into a case where there is no app available on one of your devices, and you will be stuck using a browser whether you want to or not.

Chapter 2 – Getting Started with Dropbox

Now that we have all of the technical stuff about cloud storage out of the way, it's time to focus on getting your Dropbox account up and running and making sure you choose the plan that suits you the best.

Just like with most cloud storage services, Dropbox has a free version as well as other subscription plans that offer higher levels of storage, more features and better support options.

Dropbox Plans and Pricing

I mentioned that Dropbox has a free plan and also additional plans that you pay a monthly fee for, and I would like to go over some of these plans so you can get an idea as to which plan might fit your needs. Since this book was written for individual and small business users, I won't spend too much time on the higher level enterprise plans.

For many home users, and even business users, the free plan has enough storage space and features that you don't need to spend the money on the subscription based plans. Here is what you get with each plan. I will be going over many of these features later on in the book so if something doesn't make sense, it will later.

Free Plan
- 2GB (gigabytes) of storage space
- 1 user account access
- Access from any device
- Computer backups
- Camera upload
- Document scanning
- Shared folders and links
- Dropbox Paper
- File requests
- Dropbox Transfer (up to 100 MB per transfer)
- HelloSign eSignatures (3 per month)
- Web previews and comments

Plus Plan - $9.99/month
- 2GB of storage space

- 1 user account access
- Access from any device
- Computer backups
- Smart Sync
- Camera upload
- Mobile offline folders
- Full text search
- Document scanning
- Shared folders and links
- Dropbox Paper
- File requests
- Dropbox Transfer (up to 2GB per transfer)
- HelloSign eSignatures (3 per month)
- Web previews and comments

Family Plan - $16.99/month
- 2GB of shared storage space
- 6 user account access
- Access from any device
- Computer backups
- Smart Sync
- Camera upload
- Mobile offline folders
- Full text search
- Document scanning
- Shared folders and links
- Family Room
- Dropbox Paper
- File requests
- Dropbox Transfer (up to 2GB per transfer)
- HelloSign eSignatures (3 per month)
- Web previews and comments

Dropbox also has various business plans where you can have multiple users and extra storage space. They also come with advanced sharing and collaboration tools as well as better security features. For example, the *Standard* business plan will run you $15 a month per user, and you get 5TB of storage space. 5TB is approximately 5000GB so that's quite a bit of space! They even have an *Advanced* business plan for $25/month per user that gets you unlimited storage.

And if that is not enough, they also have professional and team accounts that range from $16.58/month to $50 per user per month. These plans offer high level security, watermarking, remote device wiping, password protected shared links, lots of storage space and legally binding eSignature requests.

Signing up for an Account

Just like with everything else we do online these days, you will need to create an account before you can start using Dropbox. Then you will use this information to log into your account each time you want to use Dropbox, with the exception of the desktop client (discussed in chapter 3).

To start the process, you will need to open a web browser and navigate to **dropbox.com/basic** where you will have an option to either log on or create an account. If you don't add the **/basic** at the end of the address, you will be stuck on a page where you will need to choose a pay for plan. Figure 2.1 shows the main Dropbox website, and you would click on the *Sign up for free* button to begin the account creation process. If you click on the *Get started* button, you will be shown the subscription plans.

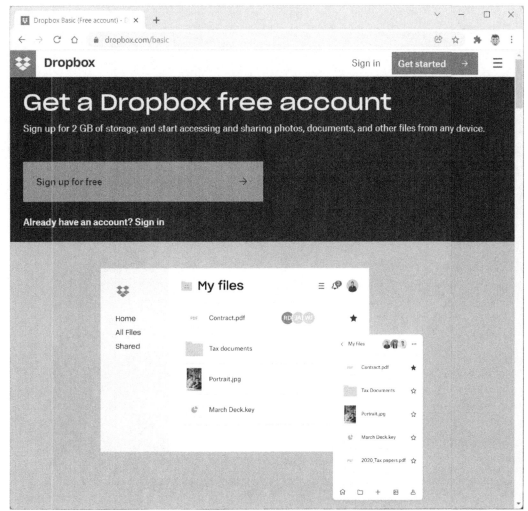

Figure 2.1

I'm sure you have noticed how rapidly things change in regard to technology. So if you see something on the Dropbox website that looks a little different from my example, that means one of these updates has happened again.

Next, you will be prompted to enter your name, email address and a password that you will use when logging into your account. You will also need to check the box saying that you agree to their terms. When complete, you can click on the *Create an account* button.

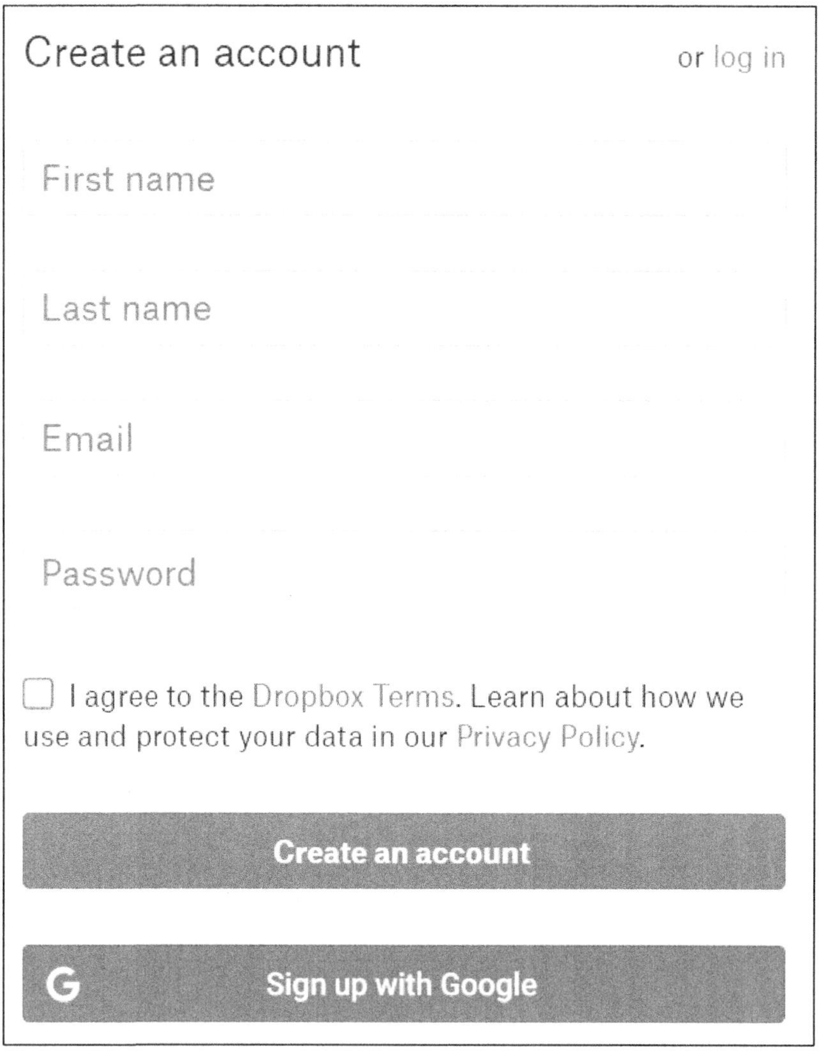

Figure 2.2

You will once again be offered the chance to sign up for a subscription based plan but if you scroll to the bottom, you should see a link that says *Continue with 2 GB Dropbox Basic plan*.

After answering a few questions, you will be prompted to download the Dropbox software, but you can skip this and just install it later if you wish.

The Dropbox Interface

Once you are logged in, you will see the main Dropbox interface and you will have a couple of files that you can open to read about getting started with Dropbox. Figure 2.3 shows the main Dropbox page with the default categories on the left.

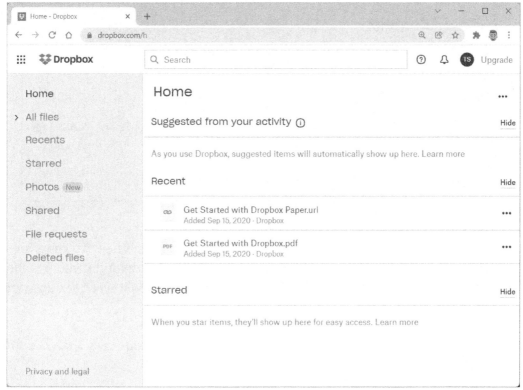

Figure 2.3

Here is what each of these categories contain.

- **All files** – This will show you a listing of all of your Dropbox folders in one place once you create some.

- **Recents** – If you are looking for a recently uploaded or changed file, you can come here to find it quickly.

- **Starred** – Starring a file is like marking it as special so it stands out. If you have a lot of files and need to find a favorite file quickly, you can mark it as starred by clicking the star icon next to the file and then come here to find it.

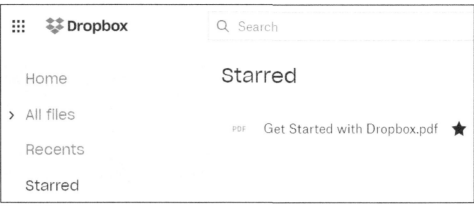

Figure 2.4

- **Photos** – This folder is used to store pictures, but you don't need to keep your photos here if you would rather keep them in a different folder. If you use the Dropbox app on your phone and have it set to sync, then it will back up your photos to this folder.

- **Shared** – Here you will find a listing of folders that you have shared with others.

- **File requests** – This is used to show any file requests that you have done in the past. This will be discussed in more detail later in the book.

- **Deleted files** – When you delete a file or folder, it will be placed in this folder in case you need to recover it.

Clicking on the icon with the 9 dots will give you access to many of the other Dropbox features (figure 2.5). I will be discussing most of these in the upcoming chapters.

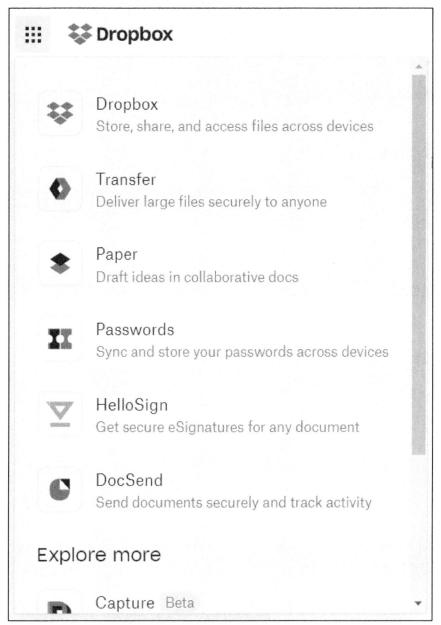

Figure 2.5

At the upper right hand side of the window, you will have the option to upload new files and folders or create them within Dropbox itself.

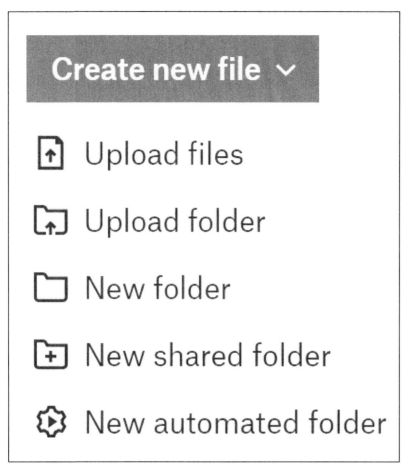

Figure 2.6

Clicking on the *Create new file* button will give you options to create Microsoft Office or Google App files on the spot and have them saved to your Dropbox. Just be sure you have a Microsoft or Google account before using these otherwise you will most likely be prompted to create one.

Create new file ∨

◆ Dropbox Paper

◆ Dropbox Paper Template

🔊 Shortcut

W Word Document

X Excel Workbook

P PowerPoint Presentation

Google Docs

Google Sheets

Google Slides

Figure 2.7

TIP

If you are interested in learning how to use these free Microsoft Office Online and Google tools, then check out my books titled **Office for the Web Made Easy** and **Google Apps Made Easy**.
https://www.amazon.com/dp/B092H828GK
https://www.amazon.com/dp/1798114992

At the very top right of the screen, you will see a few icons that each have their own purpose (figure 2.8).

Figure 2.8

The question mark icon is used to find help on using Dropbox. You can access the help center or the Dropbox community forums from here depending on what kind of help you need.

The bell icon is used to show you notifications such as when someone shares a file with you. When you have a notification, it will have a number on top of the bell indicating that it might be something you should take a look at.

The circle with your initials will show you details about your account is also where you can access the Dropbox settings (discussed in chapter 5).

And of course there is an *Upgrade* link that you can click on to sign up for one of the subscription based accounts if you feel you need any additional space or features.

Chapter 3 – File and Folder Tasks

Now that you have a better understanding of how the Dropbox interface looks and functions, it's time to start uploading and creating some files so we can get our data backed up and share files with colleagues later on.

Uploading Files and Folders

Once you have your account set up, it's time to start uploading some files and folders to your online storage. Of course it's up to you to decide which files and folders you want to keep in Dropbox based on your needs. You obviously don't want to upload anything that you don't need to share or is not important for backup purposes because you will find yourself running out of space rather quickly if you do this.

Uploading Files

To upload a file you can click on the *Upload files* link (figure 3.1) and browse to the location of the file or files you want to upload (figure 3.2).

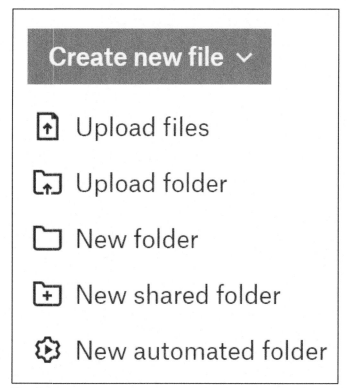

Figure 3.1

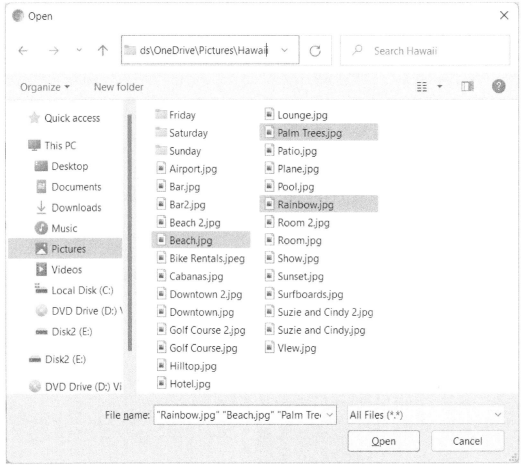

Figure 3.2

You can select the file you want to upload or select multiple files to upload at one time, so you don't have to repeat the same step over again for each file. Once you have your files selected, click on the *Open* button to have them uploaded.

Since I have not created any folders yet, I am prompted to either create one now or upload them into the main Dropbox area. If I were to just click the *Upload* button as seen in figure 3.3, they would be mixed in with any files in my main Dropbox area as seen in figure 3.4. I will be discussing creating folders in the next section and then I can move these pictures into their own folder.

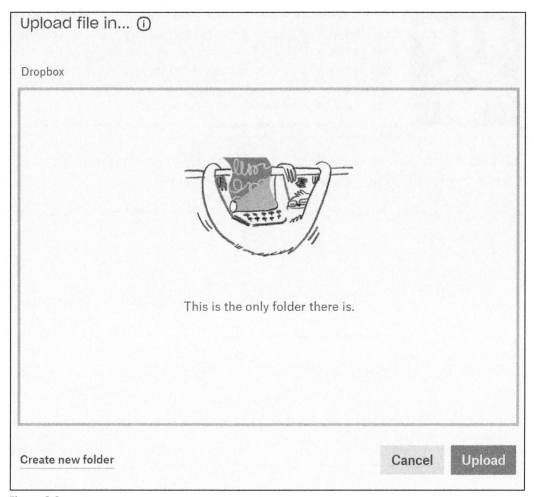

Figure 3.3

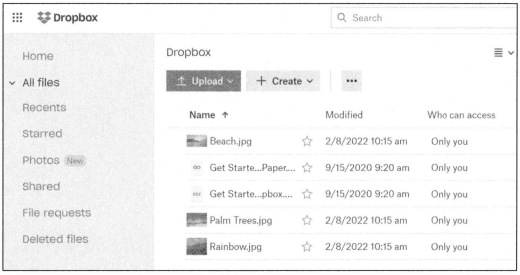

Figure 3.4

One thing you will notice when using Dropbox is that the location of the upload files and folder button will change depending on what view or folder you happen to be in. Figure 3.4 shows the Upload button above the file and folder list rather than in the upper right hand corner like you saw before.

As your files are uploading, you can click on the *upload details* status bar at the bottom to view the details about the files being uploaded.

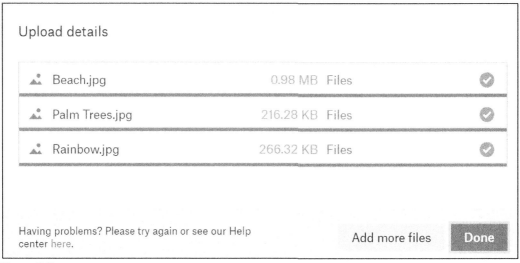

Figure 3.5

If I want to change the view of my files, I can click on the down arrow at the upper right hand side of the window and choose from grid, large grid, list and large list.

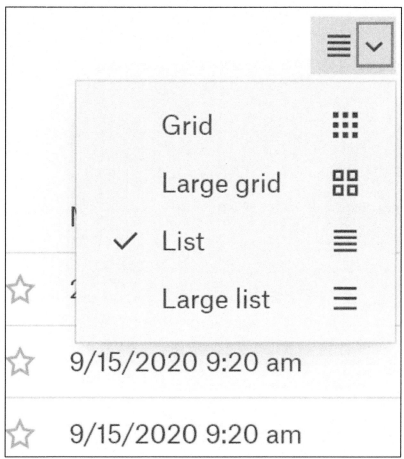

Figure 3.6

The list view will show details about each file such as the date it was modified and who can access the file. The grid view will show you more of a thumbnail or preview of the files so you can get an idea of what each file is without opening them (figure 3.7).

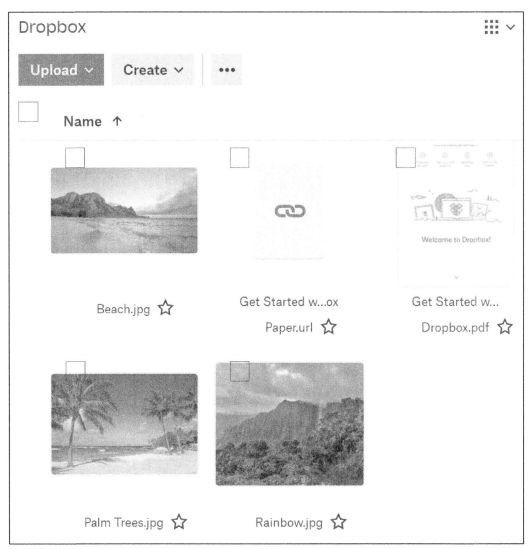

Figure 3.7

Uploading Folders
To upload a folder, you will click on the *Upload folder* choice from figure 3.1 and browse to the location of the folder just like you did for files. One difference between uploading folders and uploading files is that you can only upload one folder at a time.

But if that folder has multiple files in it, they will get uploaded along with the folder. I have uploaded a folder called PDF and as you can see from the upload details, it shows that there were two files within that folder. It also shows the name of the folder over to the right of each file name.

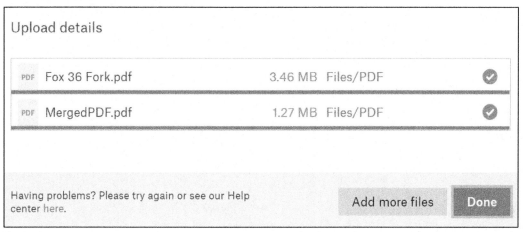

Figure 3.8

Now, what happens if I want to upload a folder that contains files AND other folders? Figure 3.9 shows the Sales Files folder I want to upload and figure 3.10 shows the contents of this Sales Files folder.

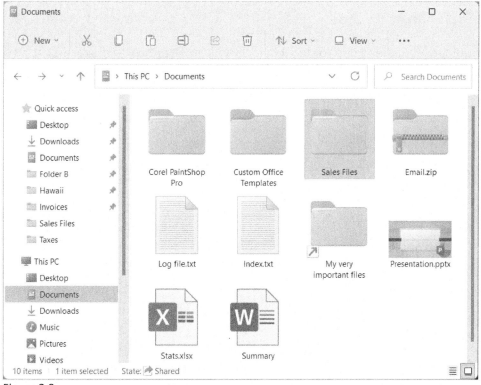

Figure 3.9

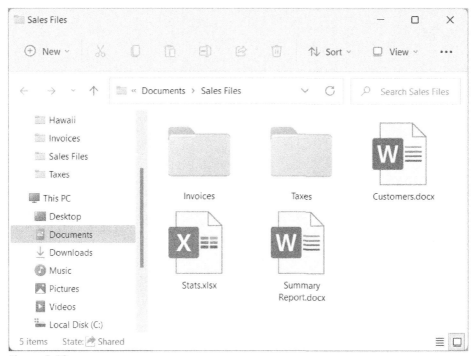

Figure 3.10

After I upload my Sales Files folder, I can open it in Dropbox and see that it also uploaded the two subfolders (Invoices and Taxes) as well as the three individual files.

Dropbox / Sales Files

Upload ∨   Create ∨   •••

	Name ↑		Modified
☐	📁 Invoices	☆	--
☐	📁 Taxes	☆	--
☐	📄 Customers.docx	☆	2/8/2022 10:48 am
☐	📄 Stats.xlsx	☆	2/8/2022 10:48 am
☐	📄 Summary Report.docx	☆	2/8/2022 10:48 am

Figure 3.11

If I look at the upload details, I can also see that it uploaded the subfolders along with the individual files.

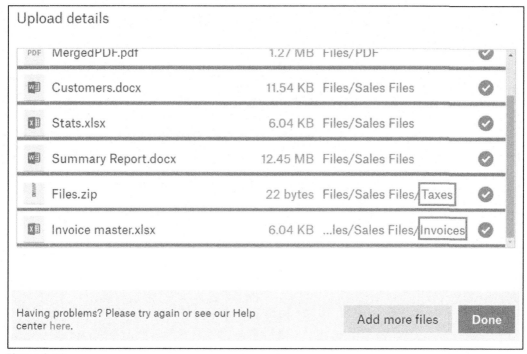

Figure 3.12

Creating Files and Folders

It's possible to create files and folders from within the Dropbox interface rather than uploading them from your computer. Clicking on the *Create* button will give you several options but for now I will be focusing on the Folder, Document, Presentation and Spreadsheet options.

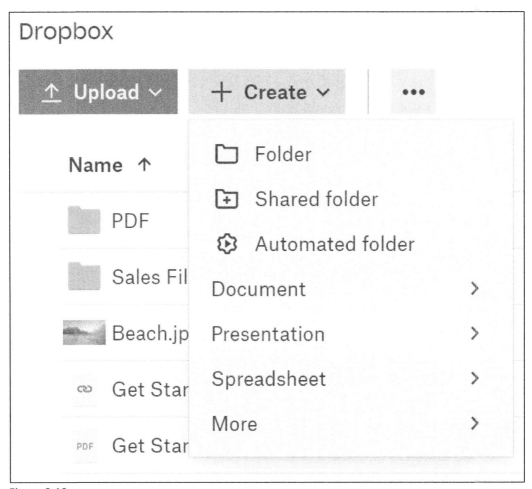

Figure 3.13

Creating Folders

I will first choose the *Folder* option to create a folder to place the photos in that I uploaded at the beginning of this chapter. I will call the folder *Hawaii Photos*. When you create a folder, you can choose who will be able to access the folder and its contents during the creating process. For now, I will choose the *Only you* option since I will be discussing sharing in chapter 4.

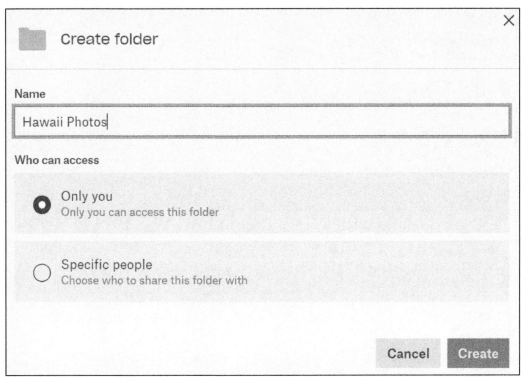

Figure 3.14

Now that I have my new Hawaii Photos folder, I can move the three pictures that should be in that folder into it. To do this, I can select each one and then either drag and drop them into the Hawaii Photos folder or click on the ellipsis (...) and choose the *Move* option and then tell Dropbox which folder I want to move them into.

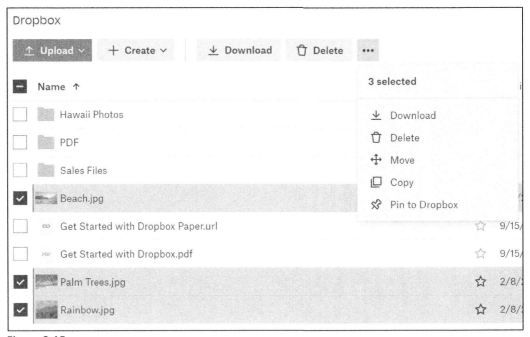

Figure 3.15

Creating Files
When it comes to creating files in Dropbox, you are limited as to what types of files you can create. It doesn't work quite the same way as it does on your computer where you can create a new text file, zip file, database file etc. on the spot.

Dropbox offers integration with Microsoft Office web apps and also Google web apps and you can use these within Dropbox and also work on these files online rather than needing to create and edit them on your computer and then upload them.

When you click on the *Create* button you have the option to create a document, presentation or spreadsheet file using either the Microsoft apps or the Google apps. Figure 3.16 shows your choices when you click on Document. You have the option to create a Word document or a Google Docs document. For the document choice, you can also create a Dropbox Paper file which is their version of an online document.

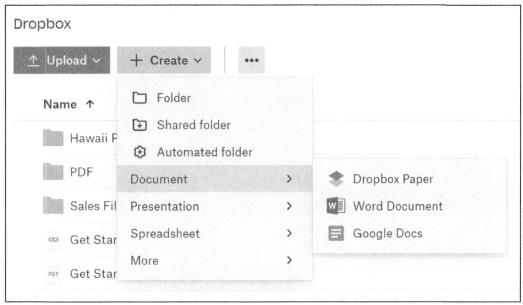

Figure 3.16

I will choose the *Google Docs* document type and Dropbox will connect to Google Docs, create the blank document and save it in the Dropbox folder where I created it from. If you are not logged into your Google account or don't have one, you may be prompted to log in first.

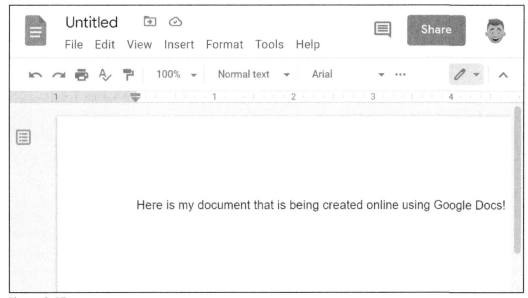

Figure 3.17

I will then be able to find this new Google document when I go back to Dropbox.

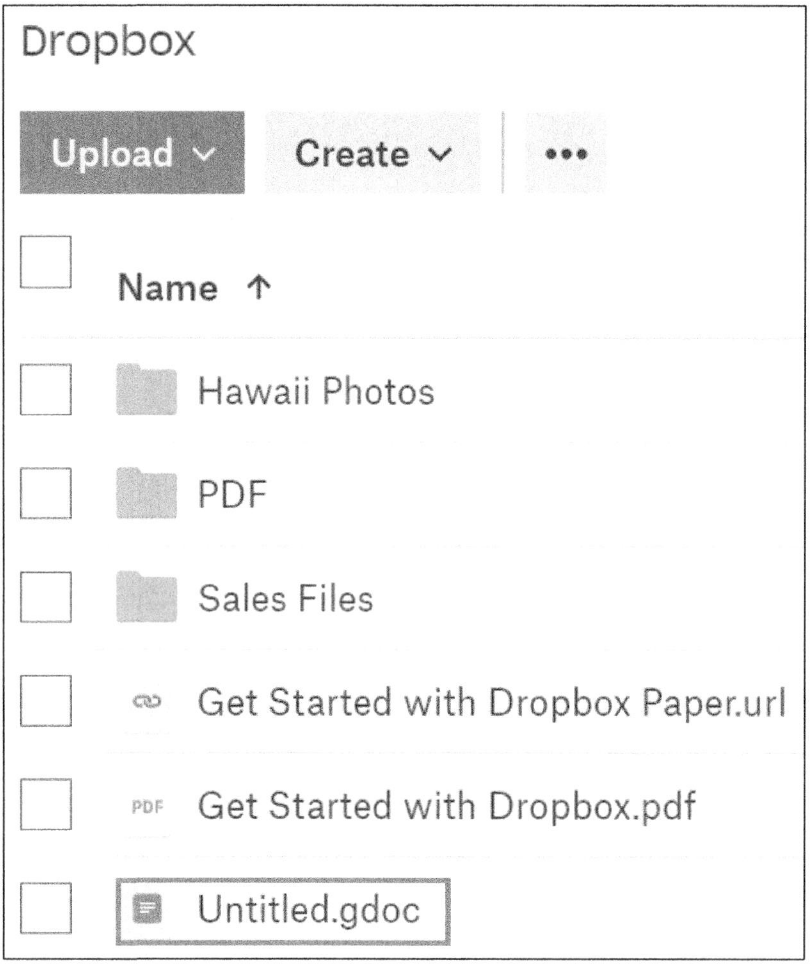

Dropbox

Upload ∨   Create ∨   •••

☐   Name ↑

☐   📁 Hawaii Photos

☐   📁 PDF

☐   📁 Sales Files

☐   ∞ Get Started with Dropbox Paper.url

☐   PDF Get Started with Dropbox.pdf

☐   ▤ Untitled.gdoc

Figure 3.18

Downloading Files and Folders

Once you start using Dropbox for a bit of time, you will find yourself not only uploading files and folders but downloading them as well. For example, if you have the need to store a local copy of a file on your computer or maybe email it to someone and don't want to share it, you can download the file first.

To download a file, simply select the file and then click the *Download* button at the top of the file list. Your web browser will then download the file to whatever location is it set to like it would any other type of file you would download from the internet.

Downloading multiple files at the same time is a bit of a different process. Let's say I wanted to download the three files in my Sales File folder all at the same time. I would first check all the boxes next to the files I wanted to download. Then I would click on the *Download* button.

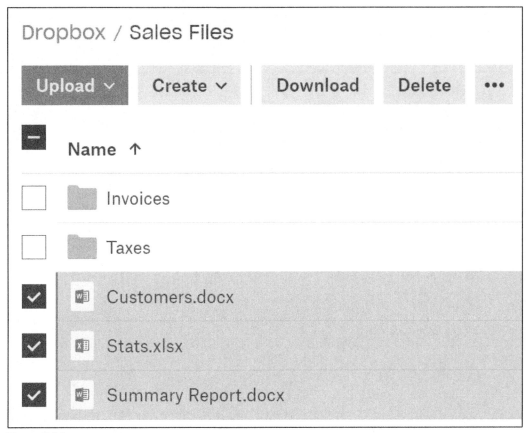

Figure 3.19

What Dropbox will do is create a zip file that contains all of the files within this one zip file. Zip files are commonly used to reduce the size of larger files or combine multiple files into one file, making it easier to email etc.

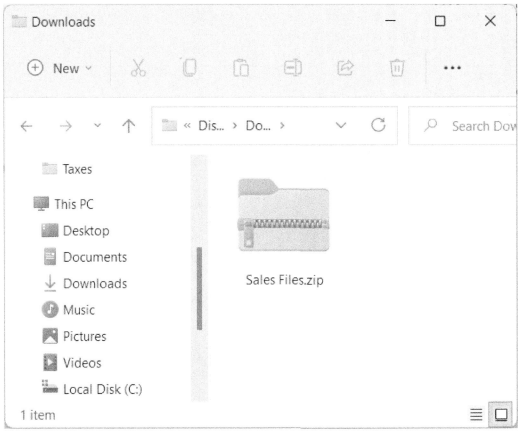

Figure 3.20

I can then either open the zip file and drag my other files out of it or right click on it and choose *Extract all* to have all of the files "unzipped" into their own folder within the folder that contains the original zip file (figure 3.22). The process for doing this on a Mac based computer will be a little different.

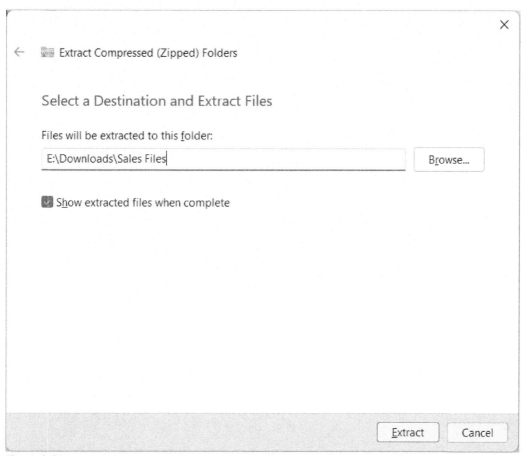

Figure 3.21

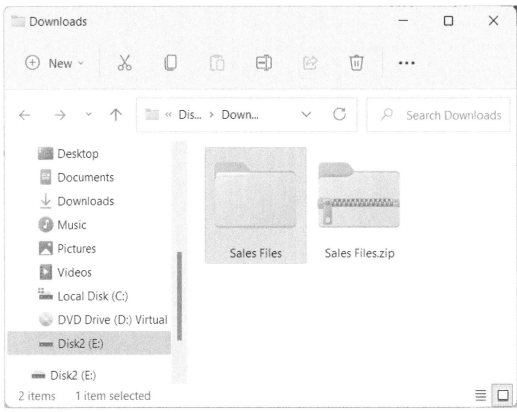

Figure 3.22

When you download a folder, Dropbox will also put the folder contents into a zip file first so everything will be in the same file. If you are downloading a folder that contains subfolders, these subfolders will also be placed within the zip file.

Opening Files Within Dropbox

I had mentioned previously that there are certain types of files that you can open within Dropbox, so you don't have to download them first to view them. You can open common file types like photos and PDF files within Dropbox so you can quickly view them.

To open a file, simply click on the file name and Dropbox will attempt to open the file within your web browser. Figure 3.23 shows a photo file opened in Dropbox while figure 3.24 shows a PDF file.

Figure 3.23

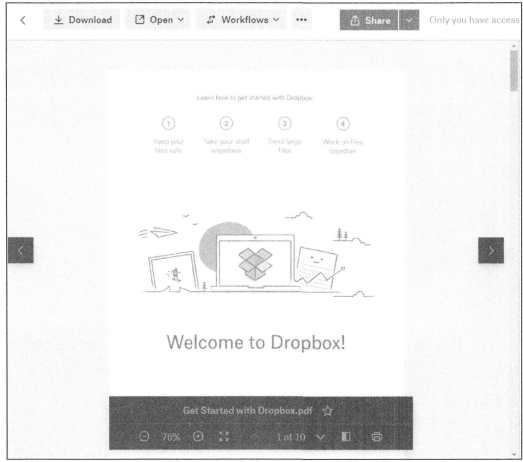

Figure 3.24

If Dropbox can't open a certain file, you will get a message similar to figure 3.25 and will have to download the file before being able to open it.

Just because Dropbox can't open a file doesn't mean you will be able to open it after downloading the file. If it's a type of file that your computer doesn't know how to open, you will receive a message from your computer letting you know it can't open the file and it will ask you what program you would like to use to try and open it.

Figure 3.25

If you are attempting to open a document, spreadsheet or presentation file, you can use the *Open in* option to choose one of the supported Dropbox apps.

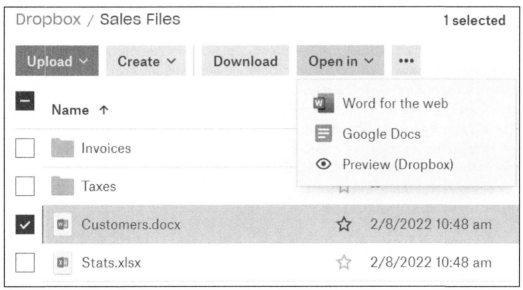

Figure 3.26

File\Folder Tags and Status

When you look a at file or folder in Dropbox, you can easily see details about that file or folder from the status area that can be opened or closed by clicking on the icon that consists of a line with an arrow as seen in figure 3.27.

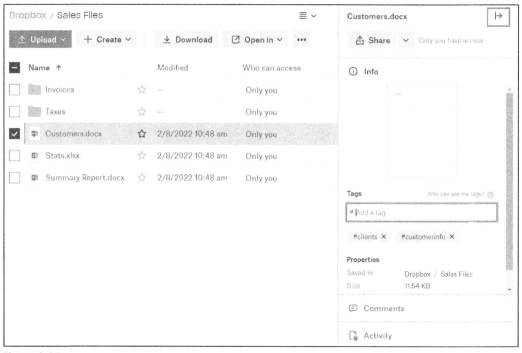

Figure 3.27

As you can see, it will show a preview of the file if possible and also show any assigned tags or comments that have been made on the file. Tags are used to help you search for files and keep things organized. You can add more than one tag to a file or folder as well. This *Customers.docx* file has two tags associated with it and they are *clients* and *customerinfo*.

The *properties* section shows you where the file is stored and also its size. The Activity section can be used to show what type of actions have been taken on your file or folder as seen in figure 3.28.

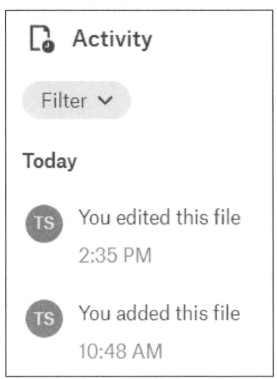

Figure 3.28

Additional Management Tasks
One other file and folder management task I wanted to discuss are the options you get when you click on the ellipsis after selecting a file or folder. These options will vary slightly depending on if you have selected a file or a folder as well as if you have selected more than one file or folder. Figure 3.29 shows what happens when you choose a single file and then click on the ellipsis.

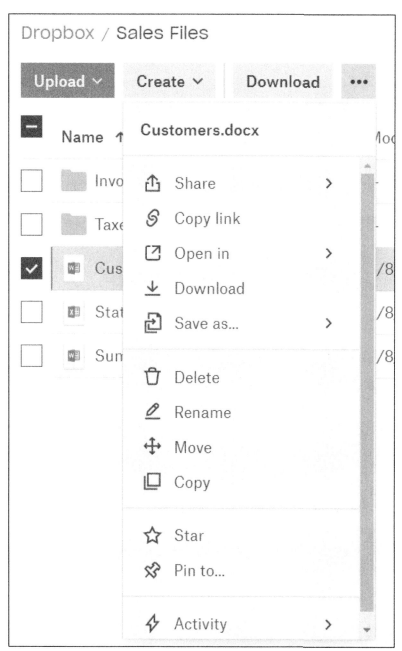

Figure 3.29

Most of the options should be obvious but I would like to go over some that might not be.

- **Share** – You can use this option to set up sharing for the file or folder.

- **Copy link** – If the file or folder is shared, you can create a link here and send it to others so they can access the file or folder.

- **Save as** – This works the same way as other apps such as Word where it will save the file as a copy with a different name.

- **Star** – This marks the file as a favorite like you would have in your web browser, making it easier to find later on.

- **Pin** – You can use this to pin a file or folder to the sidebar of another folder, making it easy to get to. Then whenever you or anyone else who has access to that folder opens it, they will see the pinned items.

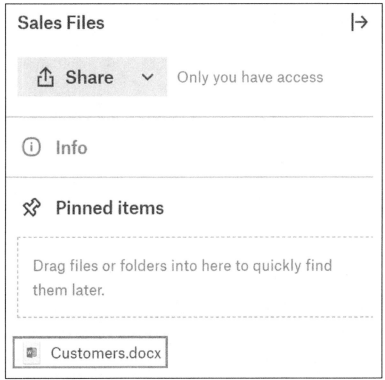

Figure 3.30

- **Activity** – You can use this section to check file activity such as version history etc. I will be discussing version history later in the book.

Searching

Once you start using Dropbox for a while, you might find it harder to locate the files you need because you will have more folders to keep them in. Fortunately, there is a search feature that you can use to help you find what you need.

The search box is at the top of the page and the first time you use it you might get a message telling you that using tags will help your search results. You might remember that you can assign tags to files to help you find them later.

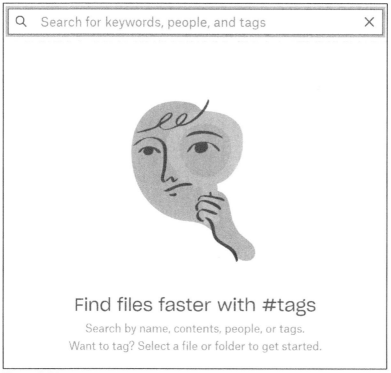

Figure 3.31

Since I added some tags to my Customers document, I will search for that one so you can see how the tags help with my search. Figure 3.32 shows the search results and in the search box you can see that I was searching in the *Sales Files* folder for the word *Customers*.

I got one result and it shows the tags underneath the file that it found. I can then open the file or take other actions on it such as move, delete, share etc. right from the search results.

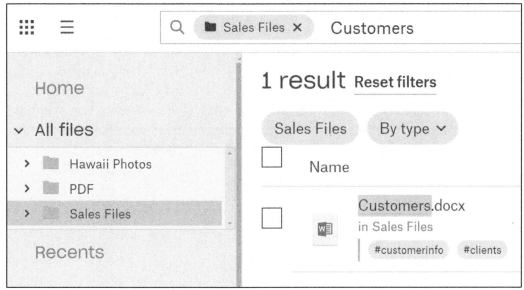

Figure 3.32

If I search from All files, I get the same results because I only have one file named customers, but you can see that this time it is searching All files rather than the Sales Files folder.

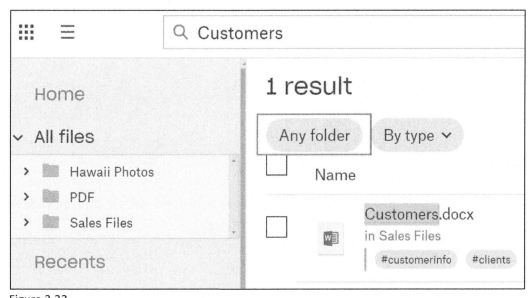

Figure 3.33

If you find yourself getting a lot of results, you can narrow down your search by clicking on the *By type* button and selecting which type of files you want to include in your search results.

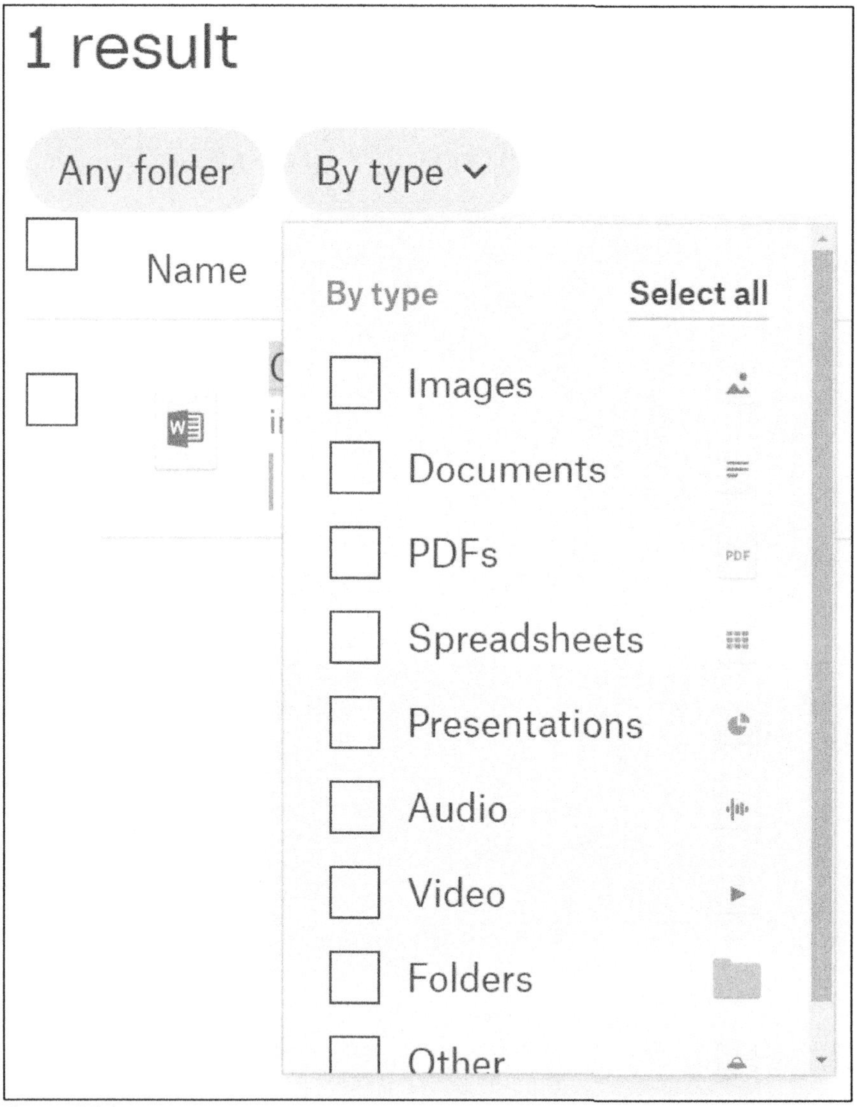

1 result

Any folder   By type ⌄

☐   Name

By type	Select all

☐   W

☐   Images   ▲

☐   Documents   ≡

☐   PDFs   PDF

☐   Spreadsheets   ⠿

☐   Presentations ◕

☐   Audio   ⁞⁝⁞

☐   Video   ▶

☐   Folders   📁

☐   Other   ⌂

Figure 3.34

When searching for folders, you might need to choose the Folders option to have Dropbox show you the proper results.

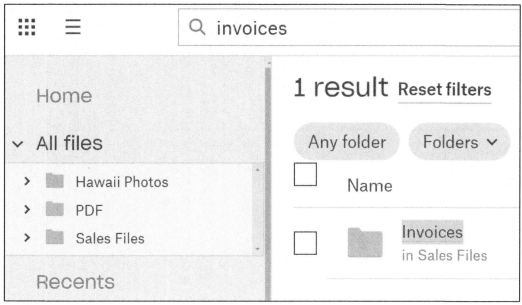

Figure 3.35

Dropbox Desktop Client

Just because Dropbox is a cloud based service doesn't mean you will need to use your web browser to manage your files. They also have a software app that you can download and install on your computer that will allow you to access your Dropbox files and folders from your computer itself and also synchronize them between your online storage and your local hard drive.

To install the client you can click on your profile icon at the top right of the Dropbox website and choose *Install Dropbox app.* Then you can click on *Download* and run the installation of the software which is pretty simple to do.

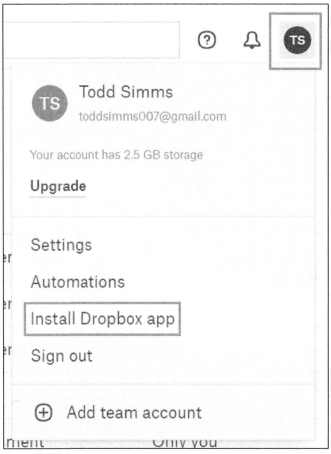

Figure 3.36

Once the software is installed, it will open your new Dropbox folder that was created on your computer. You will then see the same files and folders as you do on the Dropbox website.

 If you have a lot of files and folders that are rather large in size, then it will most likely take Dropbox a few minutes to synchronize them between the Dropbox cloud storage and your computer. And if you have a very slow internet connection, this can take quite a bit of time.

Figure 3.37 shows how my Dropbox folder looks on my computer. You can see that each of the items has a checkmark next to it which indicates that it is up to date and synchronized with the Dropbox server. The last document named **Untitled.gdoc** has a cloud icon next to it which tells you that it's a document that

was created using an online app such as Google Docs and it will need to be opened online rather than from my computer.

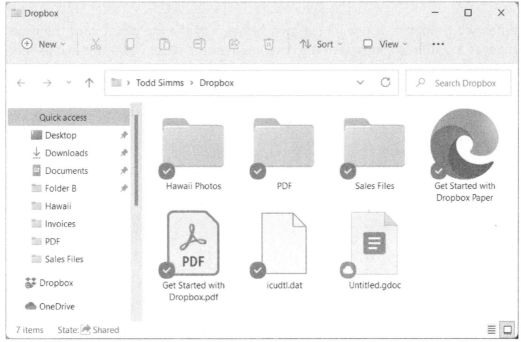

Figure 3.37

If I were to add a new file or folder to my local Dropbox folder, it would automatically be added to my Dropbox account online, assuming I was connected to the internet. If I'm not connected to the internet then the next time I do connect, everything will be synced up. If a file is changed or edited from either location, those changes will be synced up as well. If you see a file with a blue circle with double white arrows inside, that means the file is currently being synchronized.

One thing you need to keep in mind is that only files and folders that are in your Dropbox folder will be synchronized with your online cloud storage so don't go thinking your documents, pictures or desktop files will all be backed up to Dropbox. If you do want these items to be backed up, you can go into the Dropbox app preferences and then enable it from the *Backups* section (figure 3.45). One easy way to get to the Dropbox app settings is by clicking on the icon that can be found in the notification area by your clock (Windows users).

You might run into a situation where maybe your computer lost its internet connection while you were editing a file and then you or someone else had worked on that file from the Dropbox website or another synchronized computer.

This would mean you would be left with two different versions of the same file. So what happens after your computer gets its internet connection back and your Dropbox app syncs with your account?

What will happen is you will have two versions of the file and one of them will show as a conflicted copy with the date and name of your computer in it as seen in figure 3.38.

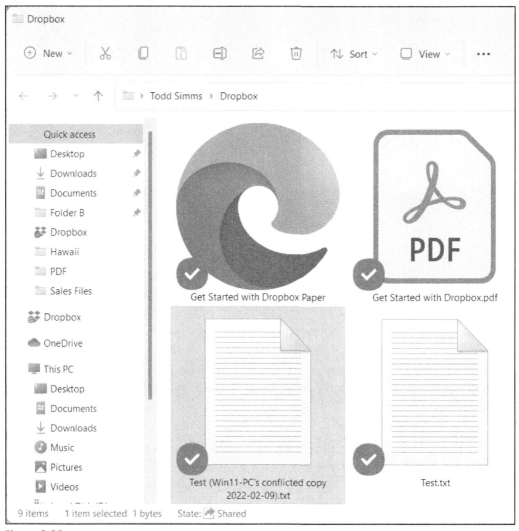

Figure 3.38

When this happens, it is up to you to consolidate the information in the two files, so you are left with the correct version of the file. Or if one of the files has the correct or more current information, you can just delete the other one.

Deleting Files and Folders

Just because you have some files stored in the cloud, doesn't mean you will necessarily want to keep them forever. Fortunately, it's easy to delete files and folders from your Dropbox online storage.

To delete a file or folder, all you need to do is check the box next to it, click on the ellipsis and then choose the *Delete* option. You can choose more than one file or folder at a time if needed.

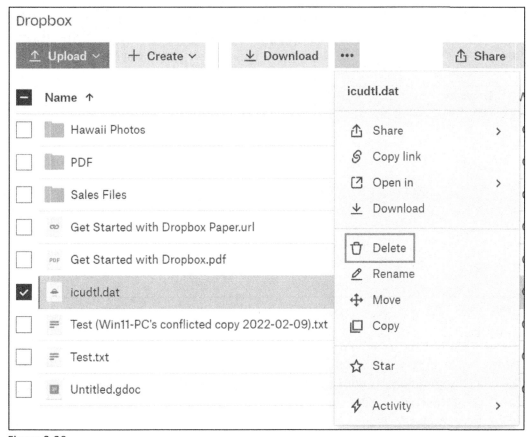

Figure 3.39

You will then be prompted to confirm that you wish to delete the file or folder by clicking on the *Delete* button.

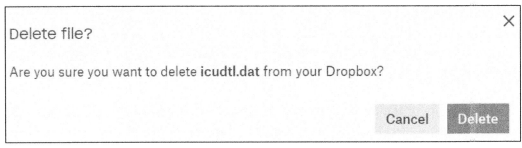

Figure 3.40

If you change your mind or realize that you deleted something by mistake, you can go to your Deleted files section, highlight the file or folder and click the *Restore* button. This will place the file back in the location where it was deleted from.

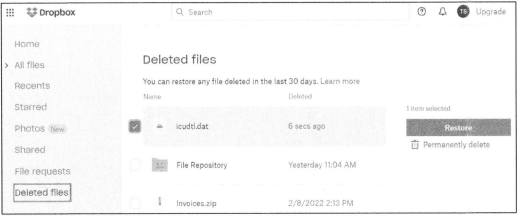

Figure 3.41

If you want to remove a file or folder for good, you can select it and then click on *Permanently delete*. Files and folders will stay in your Deleted files area for 30 to 120 days depending on your plan. After that, they will be removed for good so don't treat the Deleted files area like the recycle bin on your computer where you keep deleted files forever.

If you are using the Dropbox app and delete a file or folder from your local computer, then you will be informed that the file or folder will be deleted from your online Dropbox storage as well.

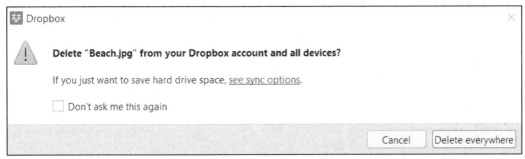

Figure 3.42

You can tell the Dropbox app which folders you want to have synced to the cloud from the app settings. To get to the settings, find the Dropbox app icon in your system tray by the clock (Windows) and then click on your initials and then on *Preferences*.

Figure 3.43

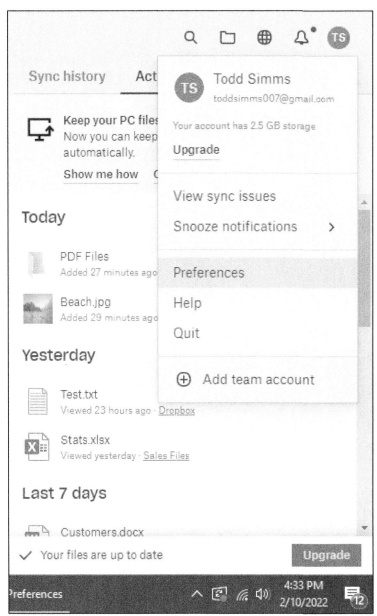

Figure 3.44

Then from the *Sync* section, click on the *Selective Sync* button.

Figure 3.45

From here you will be able to tell Dropbox which folders you want to be synced with the cloud. Note that this only works for folders and their contents, and you won't see any standalone files here.

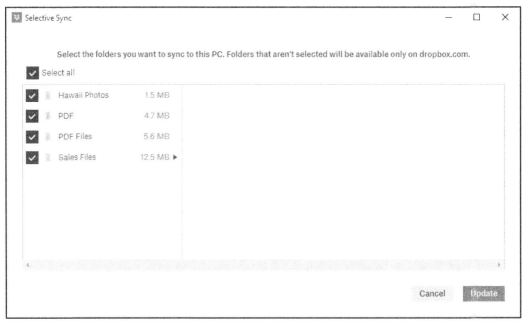

Figure 3.46

What I would suggest is if you need to keep a file or folder on your computer but don't want it in your Dropbox, you can move that file or folder out of the Dropbox folder on your computer. When you do this, you will receive a notification saying it will be moved to a different folder and removed from your Dropbox account. If this is what you want, you can click on the *Move out of Dropbox* button.

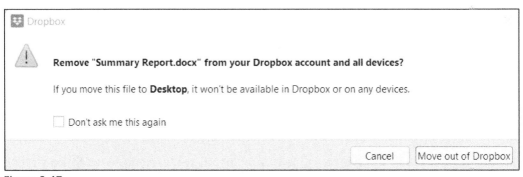

Figure 3.47

Chapter 4 – Sharing and Collaboration

Besides backup and easy access to your files, sharing and collaboration is one of the main reasons people use cloud storage services like Dropbox to store their files. If you are working on a project with multiple people and many different files, emailing them back and forth can get messy because it can be very hard to try and make sure you are working on the latest version of a file. Plus you also need to wait for people to send you an email with the file you need so you can do your part.

In this chapter, I will be discussing how to share your files and folders with other people and also how to set access levels on your files so only the people you want to make changes to them can do so.

Sharing Files and Folders
In order for other people to be able to access your files, you will need to share them first. There are different ways to do this but in the end, the result will be the same.

Sharing Folders
If you would like to create a shared folder from your Dropbox account, you can go to the *Shared* section in Dropbox and then click on the *Create shared folder* button.

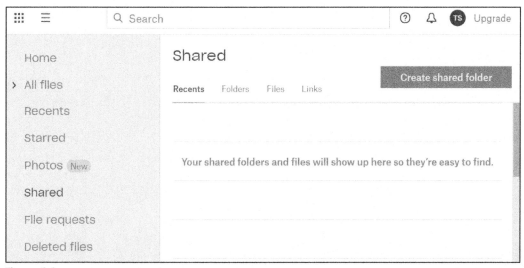

Figure 4.1

Then you will have the option to either create a new folder and share it after it has been created or you can share an existing folder. For my example, I will create a new shared folder called *Project Files*.

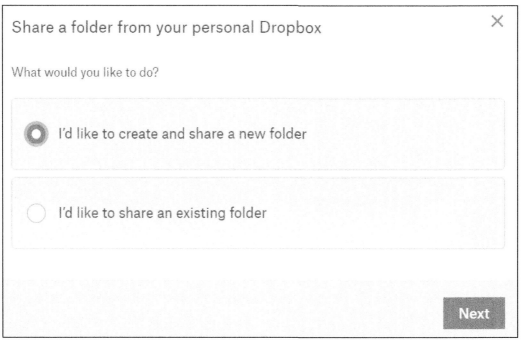

Share a folder from your personal Dropbox   ✕

What would you like to do?

    ◉   I'd like to create and share a new folder

    ○   I'd like to share an existing folder

    Next

Figure 4.2

On the next screen, I will type in the name for this shared folder and then add the email address or addresses of the people I want to share it with. I can also add a message that the recipients will see when they receive the email about being given access to this folder. Finally, I can assign them the right to edit the content of the folder or just view its content.

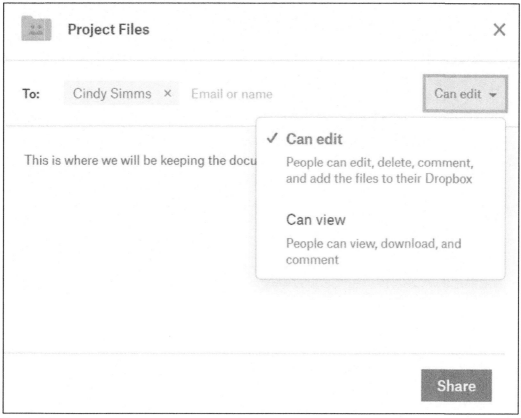

Figure 4.3

Once I have everything set, I will click on the *Share* button and my new folder will be created and the email send out to everyone that I listed. Figure 4.4 shows how the email will look for the people who were invited to access this shared folder. Then the person who needs to access the folder can click on the *Go to folder* button to view its contents. Then they will get a message asking them if they want to add it to their Dropbox account.

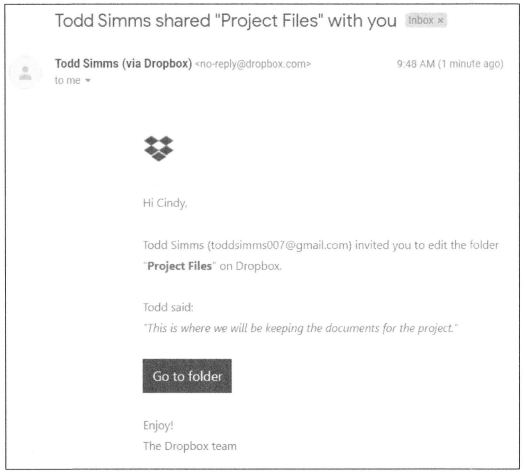

Todd Simms shared "Project Files" with you Inbox ×

Todd Simms (via Dropbox) <no-reply@dropbox.com>   9:48 AM (1 minute ago)
to me ▾

Hi Cindy,

Todd Simms (toddsimms007@gmail.com) invited you to edit the folder
"**Project Files**" on Dropbox.

Todd said:
"This is where we will be keeping the documents for the project."

Go to folder

Enjoy!
The Dropbox team

Figure 4.4

Then this new folder will be listed in their Dropbox account as if it was their own folder. They will then be able to access this folder from their Shared or All files section. If they don't want access to this shared folder any longer, they can click on the ellipsis next to it and choose *Remove from Dropbox*.

Figure 4.5

As of this writing, the Shared section can be a little inconsistent on how it works and what it will display. If you share folders using the method, I will be discussing next, they may or may not show here and you might have to manage them from their actual location. This has been a problem for many users but maybe by the time you are reading this, it will be fixed. You can also create a shared folder from your All files section within Dropbox using the dropdown menu under the *Create* button.

Now I will be going over how you would share an existing folder from its actual location. I will share my *Sales Files* folder by going to its location and hovering over the name and then clicking on the *Share* button. I can also click on the ellipsis that appears when I select the file and choose *Share* from there.

Figure 4.6

Once again, I can choose the access level and add the email addresses of the people I wish to share the folder with. I can also add a message if needed and then click the *Share folder* button.

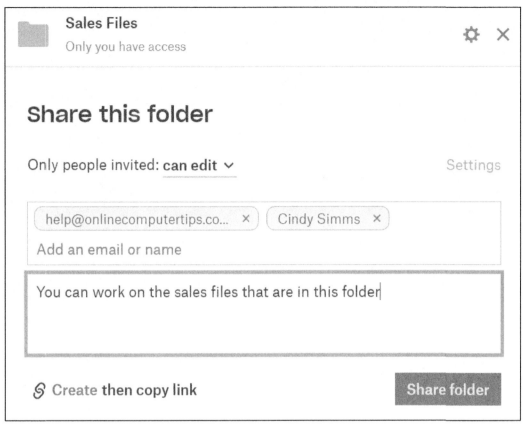

Figure 4.7

As you start to share folders, you can see which are shared by looking at the Type column. Figure 4.8 shows the two folders I just shared listed as *Shared folders*.

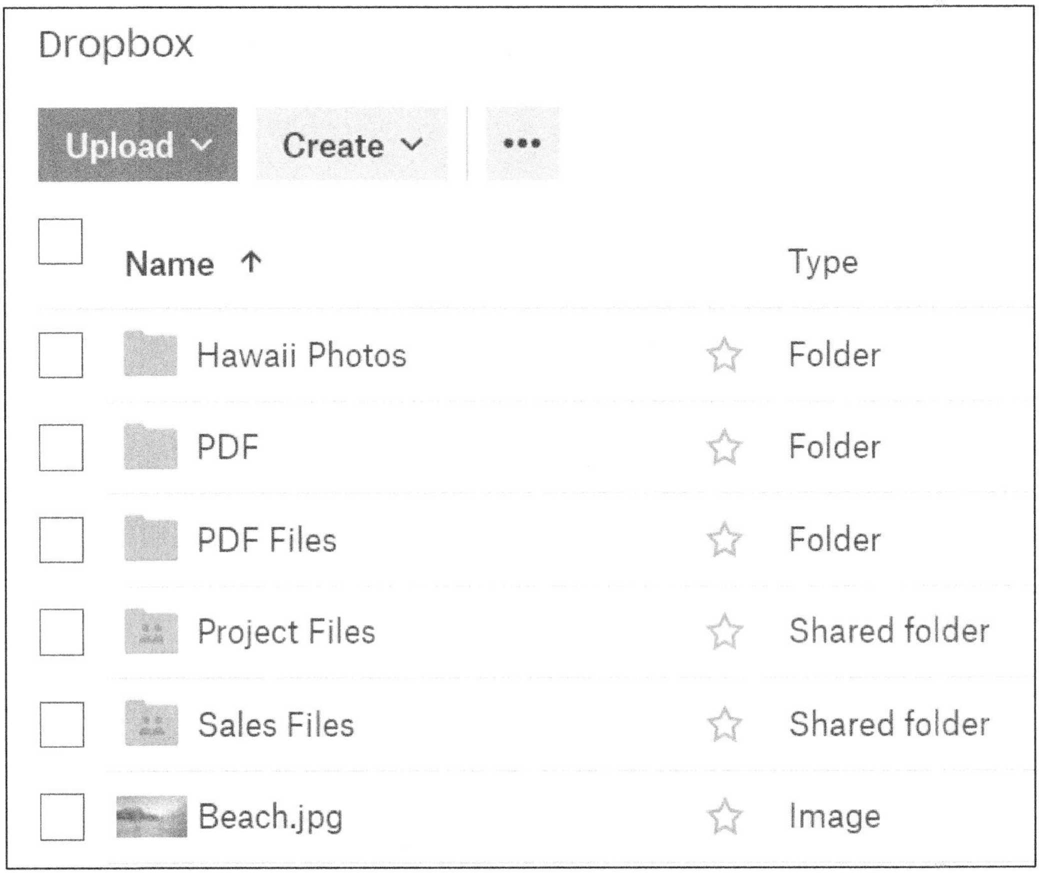

Figure 4.8

Once a person adds your shared folder to their Dropbox, they will then be able to view and edit your files, as well as add their own files and folders assuming you gave them the proper permissions to do so when setting up the share.

There are a couple of important things I want to point out when it comes to sharing files and folders on Dropbox. One of the people I shared this folder with does not have a Dropbox account so they will not be able to access my shared folder unless they sign up for one.

And for the person who does have Dropbox and has added my shared folder to their account, any files I or anyone else adds to that folder will count against their storage space. So if you have let's say 100MB of space left in your Dropbox account and someone shares a folder that has files that add up to 150MB, you will not be able to add that folder to your account.

If you would like to see what is going on with your shared folder, you can click on the ellipsis next to its name and choose *Events*. Then you will be shown a list of who did what as well as when they did it.

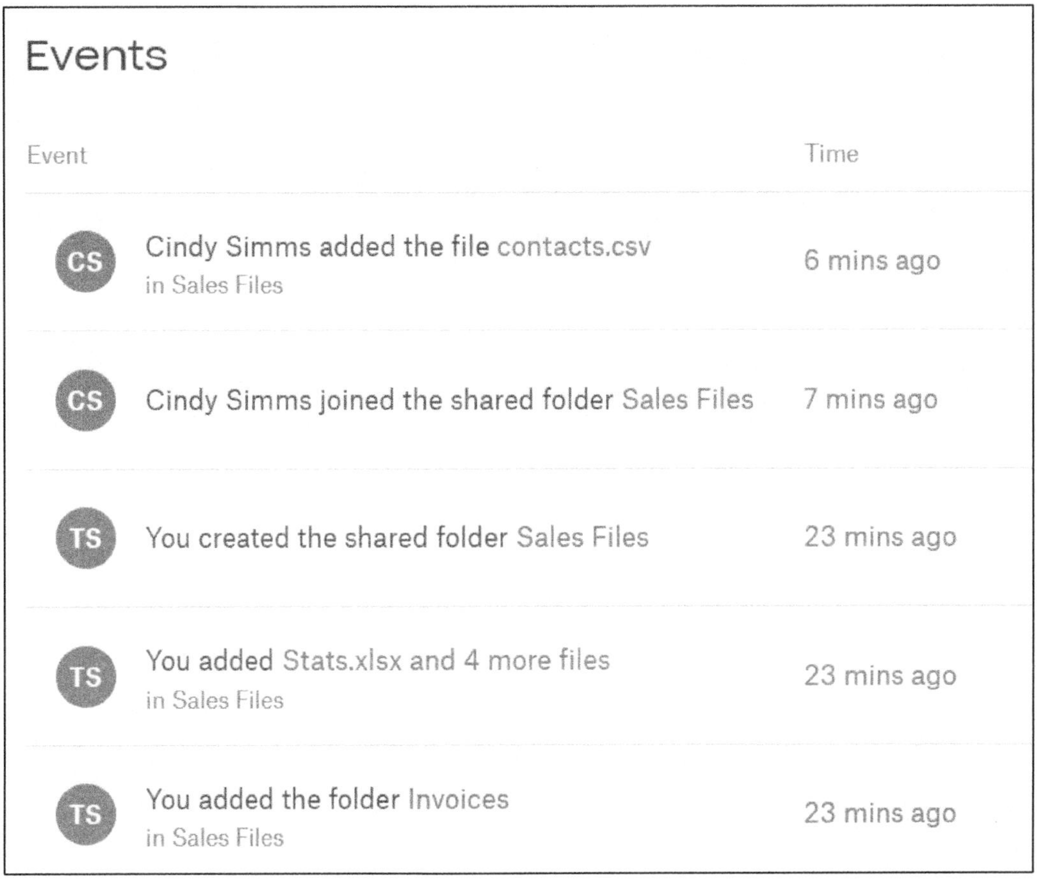

Figure 4.9

If you would like to see who has access to a shared folder, you can click on the Share button again and then click on the link under the name that shows how many people have access (figures 4.10 and 4.11). You can also change their permission levels from here as well.

Figure 4.10

Figure 4.11

Sharing Files

You can share individual files the same way you share folders and the people you share them with will be notified via email as well. When they click on the *View file* button, they will be taken to that file in Dropbox and if it's possible to view the file in a web browser, it will be opened. Otherwise, they will need to download the file before being able to access it.

Hi Cindy,

Todd Simms (toddsimms007@gmail.com) invited you to view the file "**300-ds-03.pdf**" on Dropbox.

Enjoy!

The Dropbox team

Figure 4.12

If the person wants to access the file later, they can go to their Shared section in Dropbox to see the file or go back to the email and get to it from there.

Creating Shared Links

There may come a time when you need someone to be able to view a file or folder and you are not sure if they have a Dropbox account or you might not want them to be able to edit your original file or add or remove files from your folder that you are allowing them to access. Or you might want them to only be able to add a file or folder that you share to their account rather than add your file or folder to their Dropbox account.

When this is the case, you can send them a shared link rather than invite them to have access to your shared file or folder. When you use this method, the person on the receiving end can simply click on the link to view or download your file based on what access you have granted them.

To create a link to a file for example, select or hover over the file you want to use and then click on the *Copy link* button. This will create and copy a link to the file, and the access level can be editor or viewer. For example, when creating a link to a Microsoft Office or Google App file, the access level will be set to editor level as seen in figure 4.13.

Figure 4.13

Then when the person clicks the link to open the file, they will be able to view it in their web browser if it's a supported file type as well as be able to click on the *Download* button to save it to their computer. If they have a Dropbox account, they will be able to open the file or add it to their own Dropbox account as well.

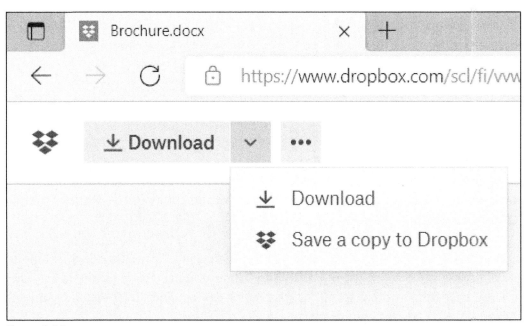

Figure 4.14

If you want to only give the recipient of the link viewer rights, you can click the Share button like you did when sharing a folder and change the *Anyone with this link section* to *can view*. Then you will click on *Create* to have a new link created that only has viewer permissions.

Figure 4.15

The recipient will still have a Download button when they open the link, and if they are a Dropbox user, they will be able to save or open the file. The thing that they can't do, is edit your original version. They can however edit the version they save to their Dropbox. If you are using one of the higher end accounts, like a business account, the Download button will actually be disabled.

If you have one of the higher level accounts such as Professional, you can click on the Settings link as seen in figure 4.15 and set things such as requiring a password to view the link as well as setting an expiration date. However, there is an option to *Unshare file* at the bottom of this screen (figure 4.16) that you can click on to stop it from being shared.

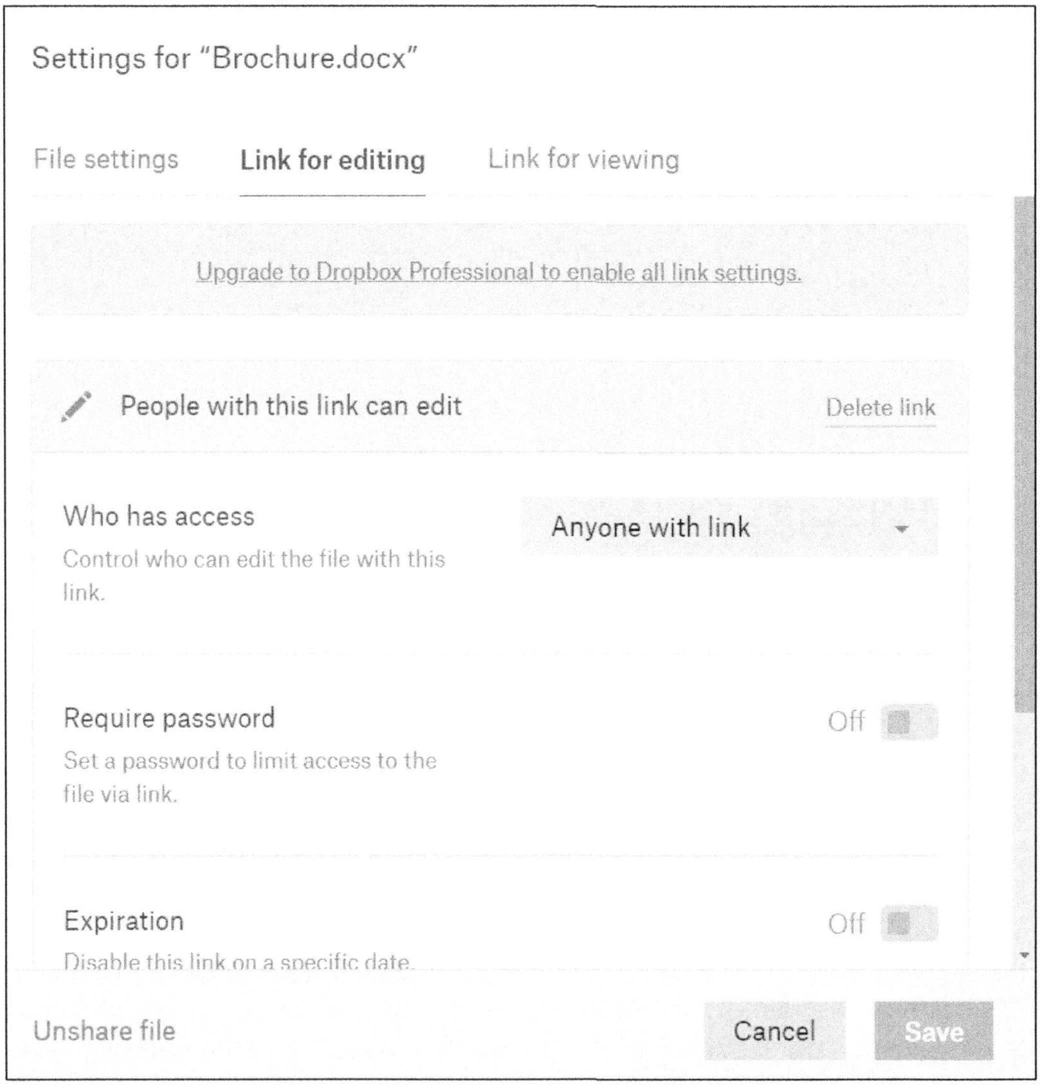

Settings for "Brochure.docx"

File settings   **Link for editing**   Link for viewing

Upgrade to Dropbox Professional to enable all link settings.

People with this link can edit   Delete link

Who has access   Anyone with link   ▾
Control who can edit the file with this
link.

Require password   Off ▮
Set a password to limit access to the
file via link.

Expiration   Off ▮
Disable this link on a specific date.

Unshare file   Cancel   Save

Figure 4.16

Checking Shared Item Changes

Dropbox makes it possible to view the history of actions taken on a shared file or folder so you can track who has been doing what to your items. In fact, you can even check the status of the changes on files and folders that only you have access to.

Over at the right side of the screen, you will see a section labeled *Activity*. If you don't have it shown, you will need to click on the icon that looks like a vertical line with an arrow next to it to expand the section.

Figure 4.17 shows the activity of a shared folder while figure 4.18 shows the activity of a shared file.

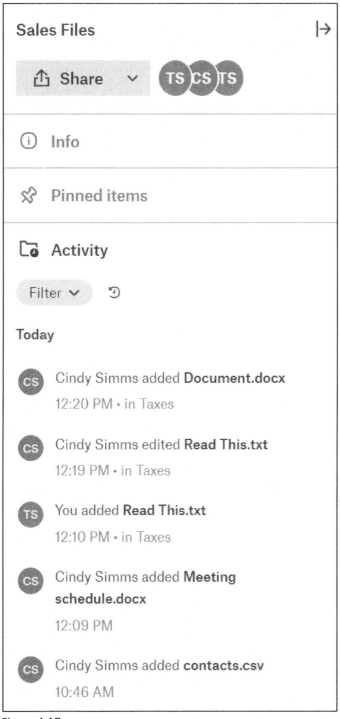

Figure 4.17

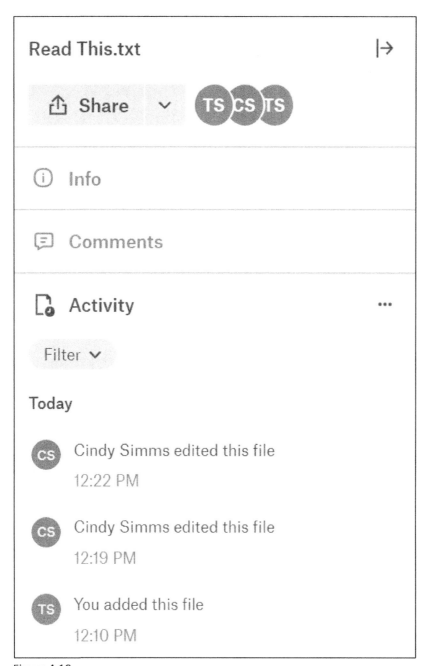

Figure 4.18

This can come in very handy when you want to know who has been working on what and also who has edited a file most recently. You can even click on the Filter dropdown to only see specific types of activity.

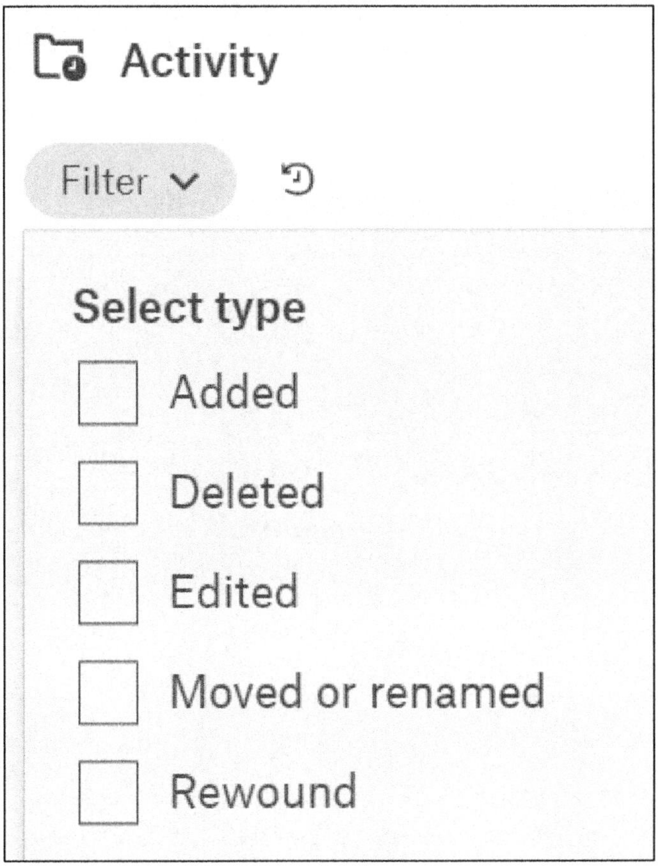

Figure 4.19

Version History

Another thing you can view which is related to file and folder activity is to check the version history of your files. When you make changes to a file or upload a replacement file with the same name, Dropbox will keep track of the different versions and allow you to see these versions in a list.

To access the version history, select the file and then click on the ellipsis like you would if you were going to check the activity of a file but this time choose *Version history* from the pop-out item that appears when you select Activity (figure 4.20).

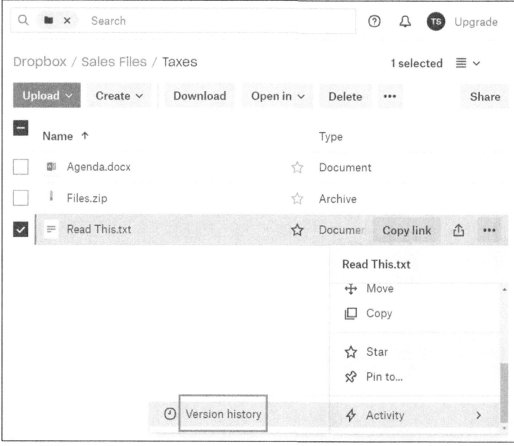

Figure 4.20

You will then be shown a list of all the different versions of the file that Dropbox has saved to your account and also who had made what changes. The file on the top will be the most current version but if you hover over any of the other versions, you will see a button that says *Restore*. If you were to click on that, you can then make an older version of the file the current version.

You can click on any of the older versions to see how it looks before making it the current version. If it is not possible to preview the document in your browser, you will need to download it first.

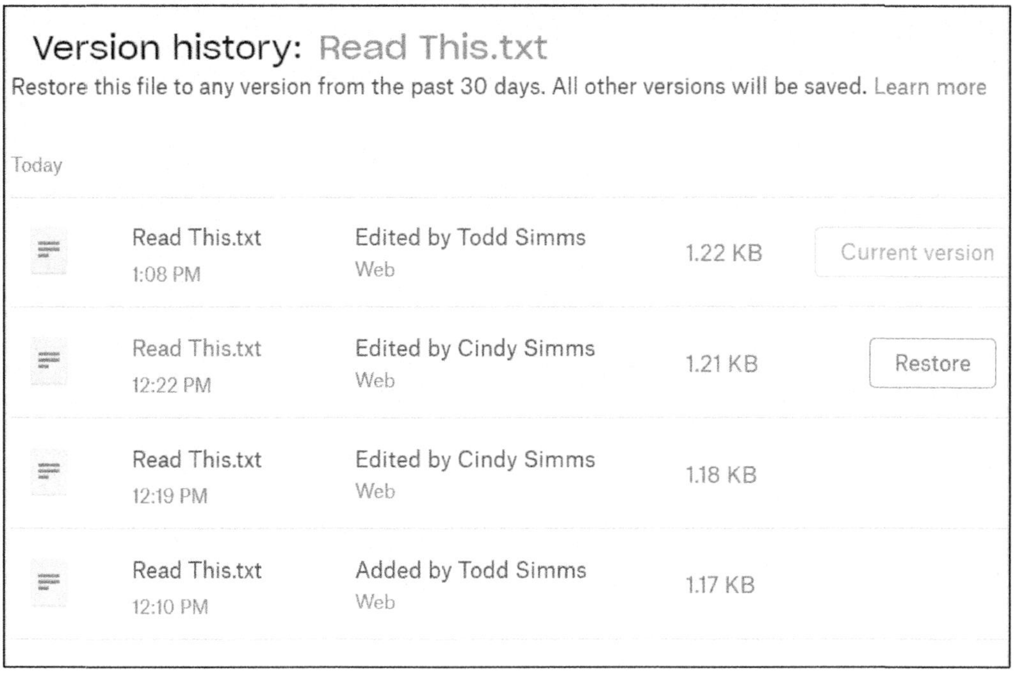

Figure 4.21

If you do decide you want to restore an older version, you will be informed that all of the other versions, including the current version will be saved.

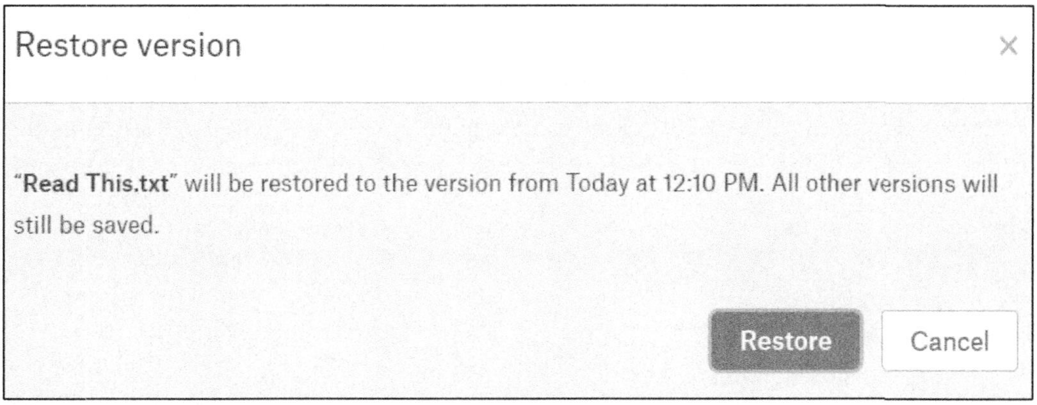

Figure 4.22

After restoring the file, it will then be labeled as restored so you know it was originally an older file.

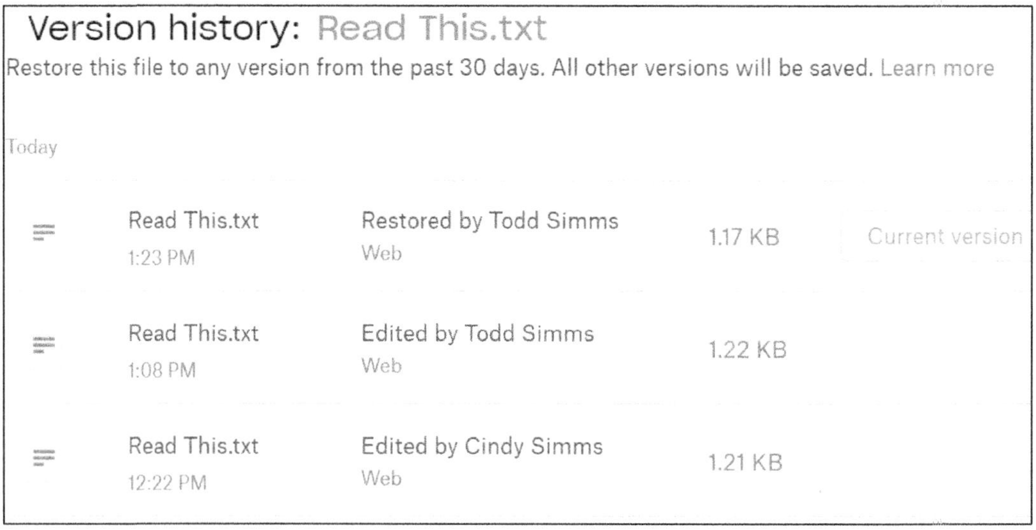

Figure 4.23

File Requests

Another nice feature that Dropbox has is that you can create a folder and then send out requests via email to people so that they can then add files to this folder. Then they can upload files to your folder without needing access to view the folder and they will not even be able to see its contents.

After you make the folder, you wish to use for your file request, you can click on the ellipsis and then choose *Activity > Request* files.

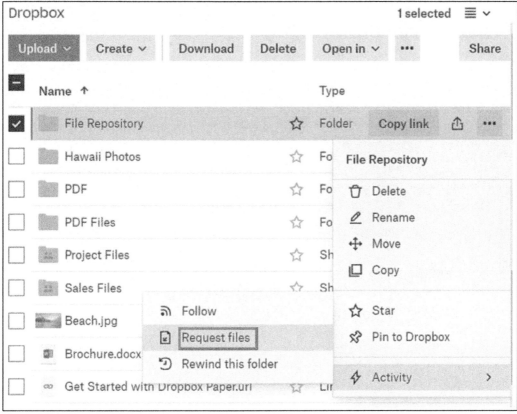

Figure 4.24

Next, you will type in a title for the request as well as a description if needed and then click on the *Create* button.

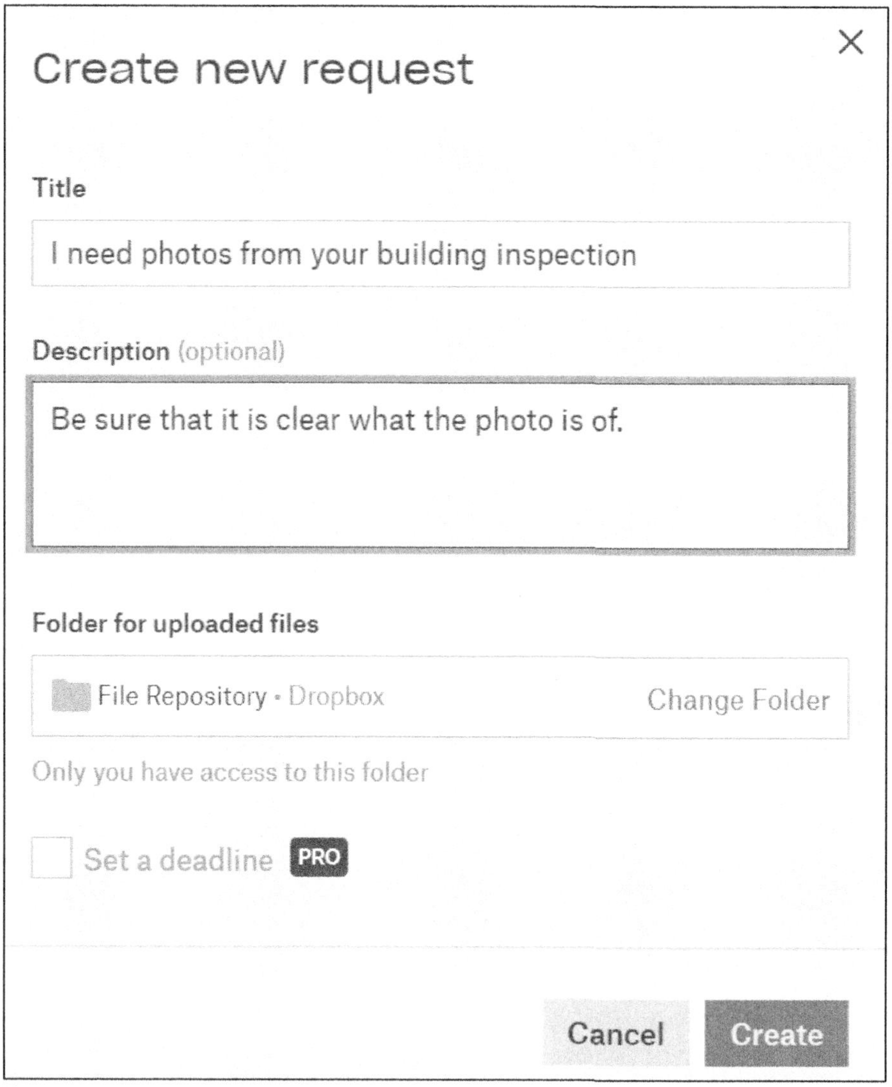

Figure 4.25

Now you will need to type in the email address or addresses of the people you want to send this request to. In my example, I will be sending the request to a Dropbox user and a non Dropbox user (jimb@onlinecomputertips.com).

Figure 4.26

They will then receive an email with a button that says *Upload files* (figure 4.27).

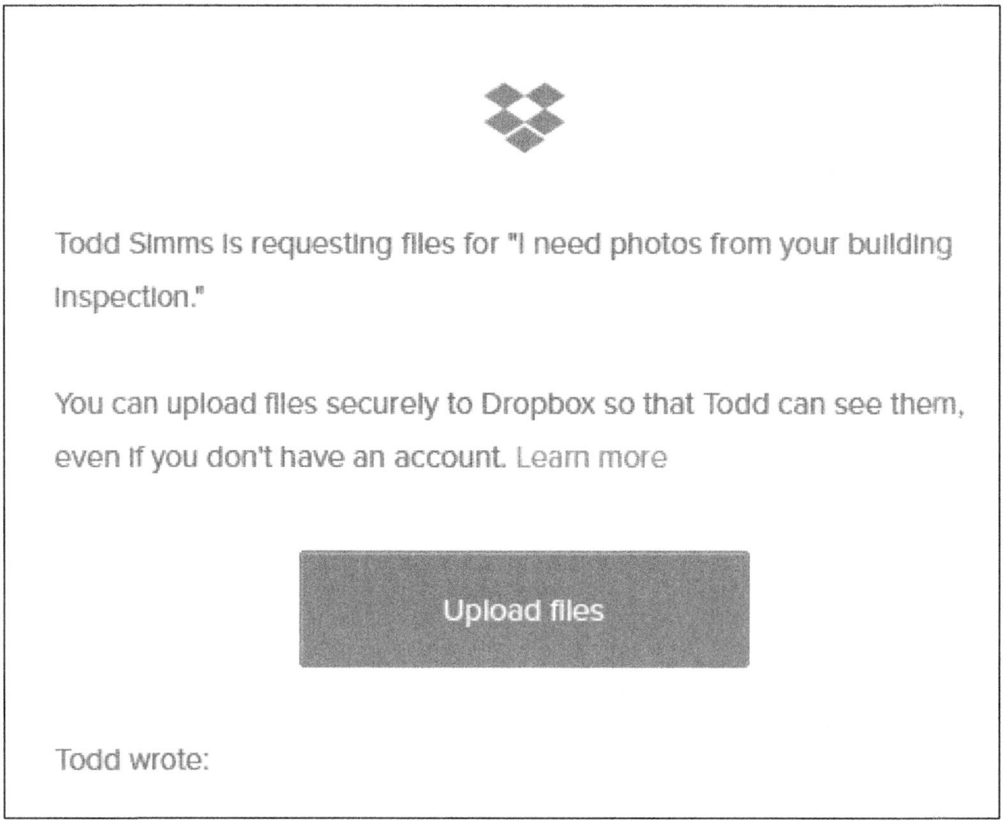
Todd Simms is requesting files for "I need photos from your building inspection."
You can upload files securely to Dropbox so that Todd can see them, even if you don't have an account. Learn more
Upload files
Todd wrote:

Figure 4.27

Then they can click the button that says *Add files* to browse their computer for the files or simply drag and drop them into the window.

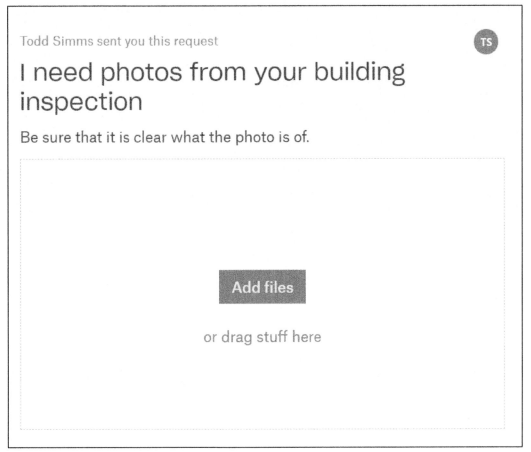

Figure 4.28

I will add three pictures to this file request and since I am doing this as someone without a Dropbox account, there is a section at the bottom to add my name and email address so the person who set up the folder will know who the files came from.

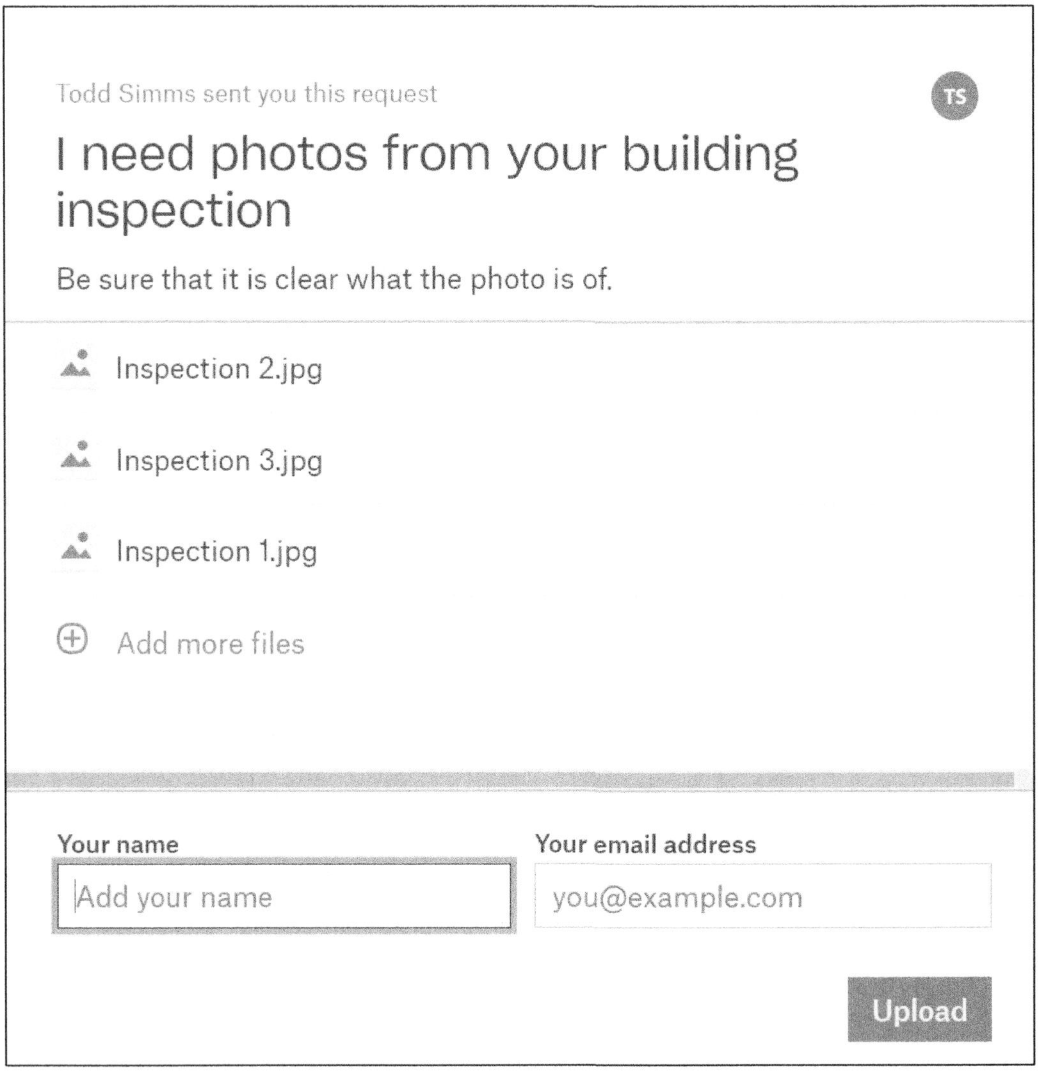

Todd Simms sent you this request   TS

I need photos from your building inspection

Be sure that it is clear what the photo is of.

⛰ Inspection 2.jpg

⛰ Inspection 3.jpg

⛰ Inspection 1.jpg

⊕ Add more files

Your name   **Your email address**

Add your name   you@example.com

Upload

Figure 4.29

After the files are updated, you can go back to your Dropbox folder and see the files with the names of the people who sent them in front of the file name.

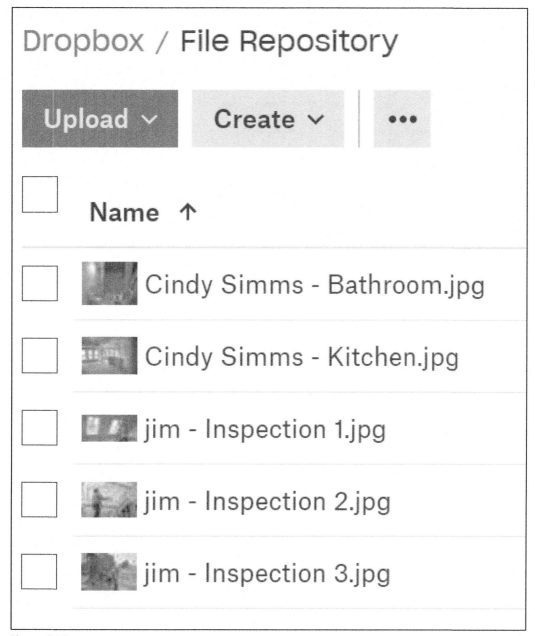

Figure 4.30

If you go to the *File requests* section of Dropbox and click on the ellipsis, you can do things such as edit the request or close it so no more files can be uploaded to this folder.

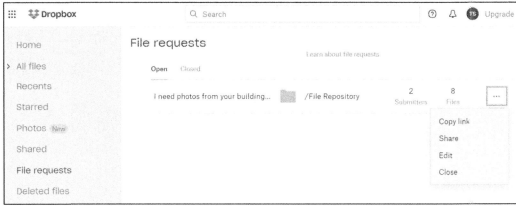

Figure 4.31

Chapter 5 – Dropbox Settings

For the most part, Dropbox works fairly well with its default configuration, but it is possible to adjust a variety of settings to fine tune how things work to possibly make it easier to use. Many people like to leave things as is or don't even know that they can make these types of changes.

I always like to check the settings for the things that I use to see how I can make them work better so in this chapter I will be going over what you can do from the Dropbox settings. I won't be going over every little detail but rather the sections that I feel are worth checking out.

Profile Settings

The first setting I will be discussing will be your profile settings. Since Dropbox is a sharing and collaboration platform, it makes sense that you would have a profile to go along with your account.

To get to your Dropbox settings, you will click on your initials at the top right of the screen and choose *Settings*. As you can see in figure 5.1, clicking on your initials will also give you the option to upgrade your account and also shows how much online storage space your account has access to.

Figure 5.1

 One other thing you should take note of from figure 5.1 is the bell icon next to your initials. This is used to show you notifications about your account such as when somebody leaves a comment or adds a file. It's also used by Dropbox to send you tips and other information about your account.

Your profile settings will be listed in the *General* section and here is where you can change things such as your name, email, language, time zone and so on. You can even add a photo of yourself if you do not want your initials to be your profile picture.

Personal account

General   Plan   Security   Notifications   Connected apps   Default apps

Basics

Photo	TS	Edit
Name	Todd Simms	Edit
Personal email	toddsimms007@gmail.com	Edit
Link your team account Your accounts will stay separate, but you can easily switch between them and access both from any device.	**Link accounts**	

Preferences

Language	English (United States)	Edit
Date format	MM / DD / YYYY ⌄	

Figure 5.2

To make a change to one of these settings, all you need to do is click on the *Edit* link next to it and enter the new information. For example, if I wanted to change my profile picture, I would click on *Edit* and then either upload a photo from my computer or use one that I have stored in Dropbox.

Figure 5.3

Now my new profile picture is shown where my initials used to be.

Figure 5.4

If you scroll down in this section, you will see some other more advanced settings that are not profile related but might be of interest to you.

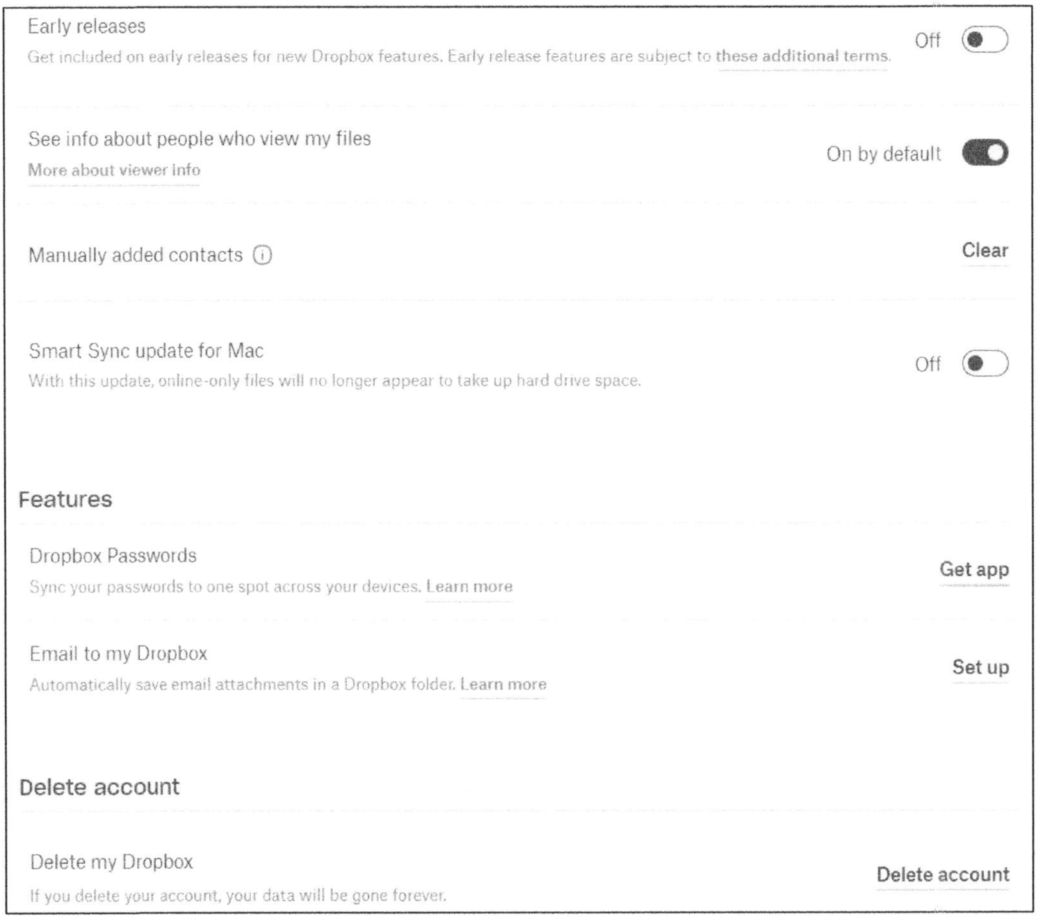

Early releases | Off
Get included on early releases for new Dropbox features. Early release features are subject to these additional terms.

See info about people who view my files | On by default
More about viewer info

Manually added contacts ⓘ | Clear

Smart Sync update for Mac | Off
With this update, online-only files will no longer appear to take up hard drive space.

Features

Dropbox Passwords | Get app
Sync your passwords to one spot across your devices. Learn more

Email to my Dropbox | Set up
Automatically save email attachments in a Dropbox folder. Learn more

Delete account

Delete my Dropbox | Delete account
If you delete your account, your data will be gone forever.

Figure 5.5

Here is what these features will do.

- **See info about people who view my files** – This allows you to see when someone is actually looking at one of your files in real time.

- **Smart Sync update for Mac** – This can be used to make files online only so you can save hard drive space on your Mac based computer.

- **Dropbox Passwords** – This is a password manager feature that can store website passwords and sync them between all of your devices once configured on each device.

- **Email to my Dropbox** – If you tend to save your email attachments to your Dropbox more than your computer then you can use this feature to have these attachments saved there automatically (discussed in chapter 7).

- **Delete account** – If you decide you do not want to be a Dropbox user any longer, then you can come here to delete your account. Just be sure to sync any files you want to keep to your computer because all of your online data will be deleted along with your account.

Security

For those who are concerned about the safety of their data and their account, you can check out the Security section to improve the security of your account and check for any security related issues.

Here are some of the features available to you in the Security settings.

- **Security checkup** – Dropbox will walk you through a 4 step process to check the security settings of your account. It's similar to checking all of the security settings manually but this will walk you through them step by step instead.

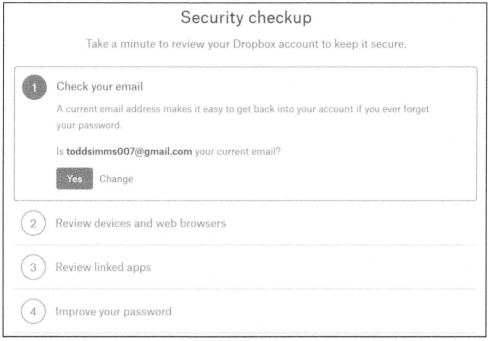

Figure 5.6

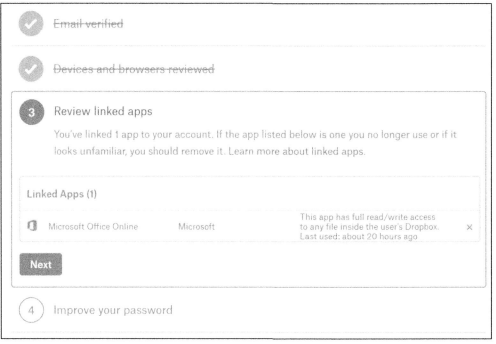

Figure 5.7

- **Password** – If you feel your password needs to be stronger or want to change it for any other reason, you can do so from here.

- **Two-step verification** – Enabling this will require you to enter a code that will be sent to your phone before logging in to your Dropbox account on your computer as well as your password.

- **Web browsers and devices** – This will show you what web browsers and devices are logged in with your account. If you see something that doesn't look right, you can click the trash can icon next to it to have the listed computer disconnected and unlinked from your account. If this does happen, I would change my password right afterward.

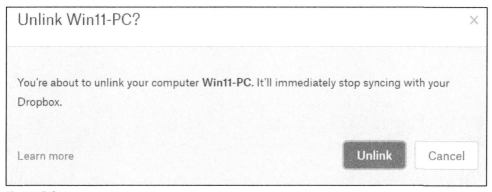

Web browsers

These browsers are currently signed in to your personal Dropbox account.

Browser	Location	Most recent activity	
Chrome on Windows	Bellingham, Washington	Current session ⓘ	
Chrome on Windows	Bellingham, Washington	26 minutes ago ⓘ	🗑

Devices

These devices are linked to your personal Dropbox account.

Device name	Location	Most recent activity	
Win11-PC	Bellingham, Washington	in the last hour ⓘ	🗑

Figure 5.8

Unlink Win11-PC? ✕

You're about to unlink your computer **Win11-PC**. It'll immediately stop syncing with your Dropbox.

Learn more   **Unlink**   Cancel

Figure 5.9

- **Paper mobile devices** – If you use Dropbox Paper (discussed in Chapter 7) and want to unlink your mobile device from that service, you can do so from here.

Notifications

Earlier in this chapter, I mentioned the notification bell icon which is used to show you messages about your account activity and other Dropbox promotional messages. Dropbox will also send you emails about your account status and other non-account items such as new features and tips on how to use Dropbox itself.

If you are not the type who likes getting bombarded with email, then you can go to the notifications settings and uncheck any of the types you do not want to be emailed about.

As you can see in figure 5.10, there are quite a few categories for notification emails that can be sent out and then are broken down into alerts, news and files.

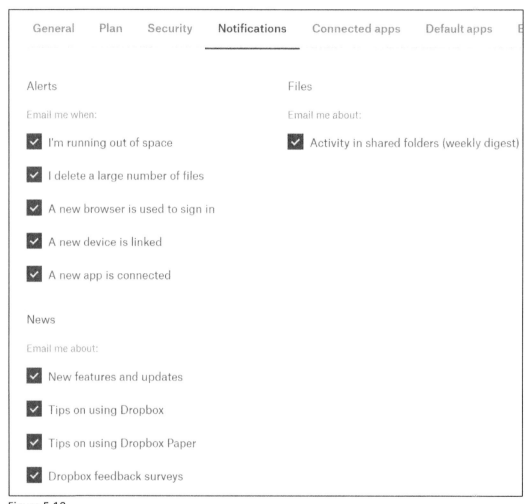

Figure 5.10

To disable any of these notification types, simply uncheck the box next to it. I would make sure you really want to uncheck anything under alerts before doing so because you might miss out on some important information about your account.

Connected Apps

Dropbox has the ability to integrate other third party apps such as Microsoft Office, Google Docs, Zoom etc. into your account so you can use them together as if they were part of the same app. The connected apps section is where you can go to see what apps you have connected as well as see what additional apps are available to use with Dropbox.

When you go to this section, you will see what apps you already have connected such as Microsoft Office Online in my case. You can then add additional apps to your account from the App Center.

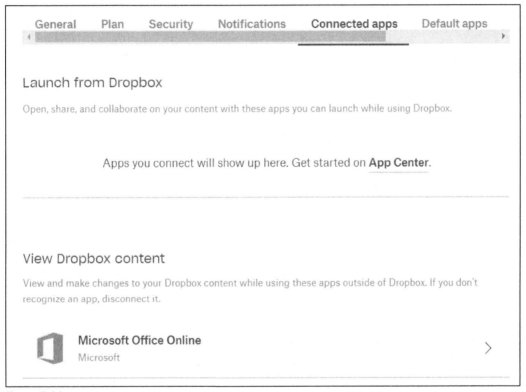

Figure 5.11

Once you find an app that you want to use with Dropbox, you will need to see if it has an option to connect as seen in figure 5.12. Some apps are easy to add by clicking on the *Connect* button while others will take some additional steps on your part to get connected.

Slack
Slack Technologies Inc

Connect • • •

Bring Slack conversations and Dropbox content together to keep teams in sync.

Keep your Dropbox content and Slack conversations together so your team can stay on the same page and find information easily.

- Start a Slack conversation within Dropbox to discuss changes or updates to shared content.
- Send files to individuals or Slack channels directly from Dropbox to easily share your work.
- See what Dropbox content was shared to Slack from the Dropbox file activity to learn how your team is collaborating.

Figure 5.12

You will receive a few prompts letting you know how what will happen when the app is connected and also what permissions will be required in order to let the app access your Dropbox account.

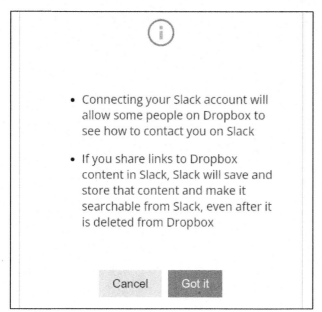

Figure 5.13

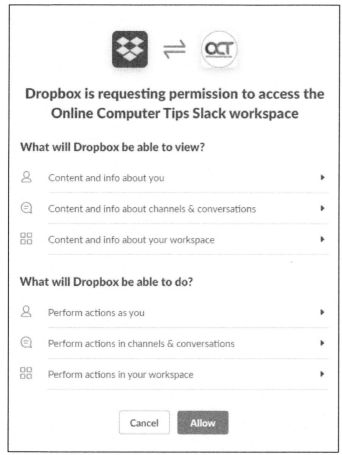

Figure 5.14

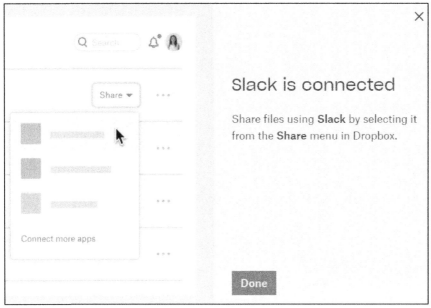

Figure 5.15

Once you get your new app connected, it will show up under your connected apps.

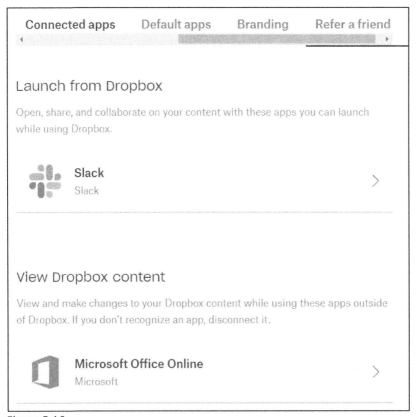

Figure 5.16

Default Apps

Unlike the connected apps where you decide what apps are used with your Dropbox account, there are also default apps that come built into Dropbox itself. These apps might vary depending on what type of Dropbox account you are using and if and when Dropbox adds or removes any of these default apps.

Figure 5.17 shows that I can make a choice as to what app opens a certain type of file. For example, to open an Excel spreadsheet file I can have Dropbox either view it on the Dropbox website which is the default, or I can have it opened with Excel for the web or Google Sheets. You can change the default app for any one of these file types from this section.

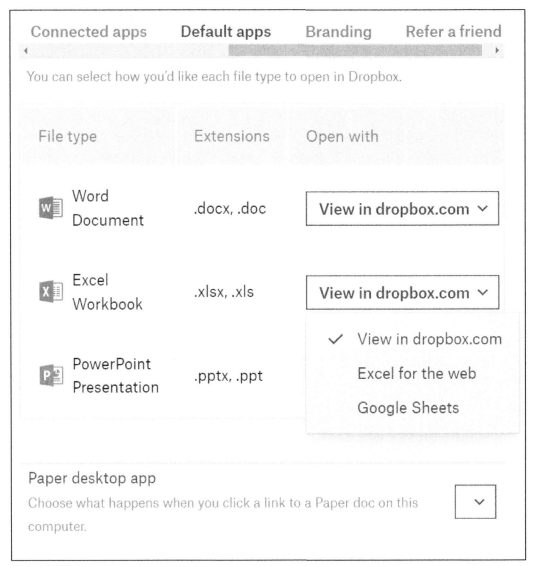

Figure 5.17

At the bottom, I have a choice for Dropbox Paper documents, and I can either have them opened in the Paper desktop app or from the Dropbox website.

Chapter 6 - Using Dropbox on Your Smartphone

Since many people use their smartphones as much as or more than their computers, it makes sense that you would want to access your Dropbox files from your phone as well. Plus your phone will have an internet connection wherever you may be (for the most part) making it handy for working with Dropbox when you can't connect from your computer.

Installing the Dropbox App
It is possible to access your Dropbox account from a web browser on your smartphone but that is not very practical because of the screen size and the way the website version of Dropbox functions. Thankfully, there is an app that you can install on your phone that makes using Dropbox almost as easy as it is on your home computer.

To install the app, simply go to the App Store (iPhones) or Play Store (Android devices) and do a search for Dropbox. Keep in mind that you might find similar apps such as Dropbox Paper or other apps that sound like they might be related to Dropbox. What you should look for is the Dropbox icon and also makes sure the app developer is Dropbox, Inc. as seen in figure 6.1.

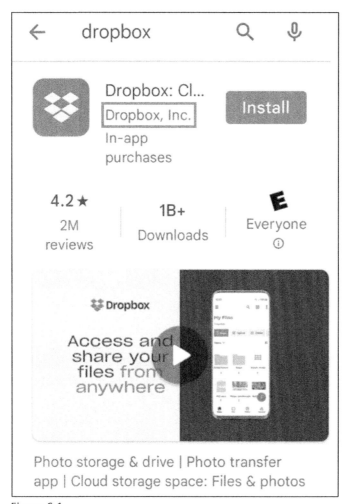

Figure 6.1

Then you would simply install the app like you would any other app on your phone. When you open it the first time you might get prompted to back up the photos on your phone or connect to your desktop computer. If you just want to get into the app you can tap on *Skip*.

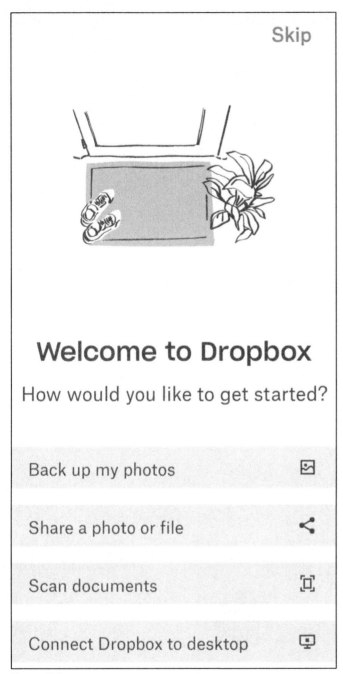

Figure 6.2

The Dropbox App Interface

Once you are in the app, you will notice that things look familiar and very similar to the Dropbox website that you use on your computer. You will have all of your files and folders shown in a similar layout to the website as well. If you were to click on the three vertical dots next to a file or folder, you would see a menu similar to figure 6.4.

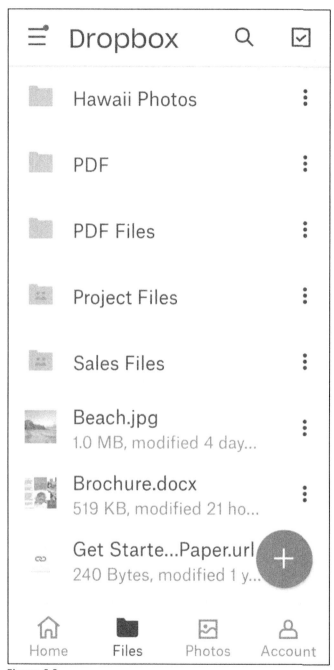

Figure 6.3

From here you can do many of the same things with your files and folders as you do from the website such as share, rename, move or delete them.

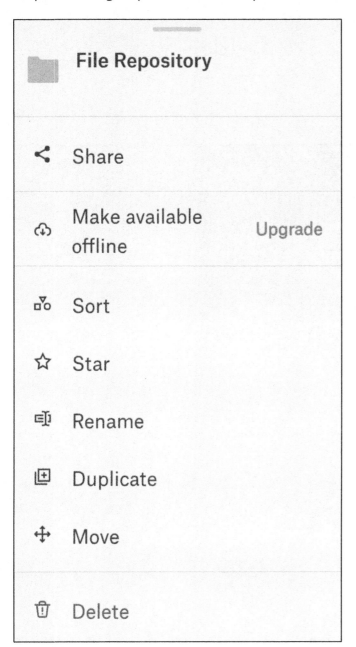

Figure 6.4

Tapping on *Photos* at the bottom of the screen will show you the pictures that you have in your Dropbox folders in one location, sorted by date. The dates used might differ from when they were uploaded to Dropbox depending on the date meta information contained in the image files.

Figure 6.5

Tapping on the three horizontal bars at the upper left side of the screen will bring you to your account information screen where you can access the app settings and view notifications. Figure 6.7 shows how the notifications screen will look.

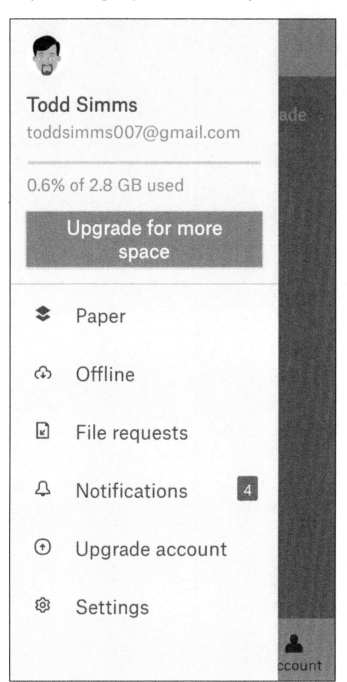

Figure 6.6

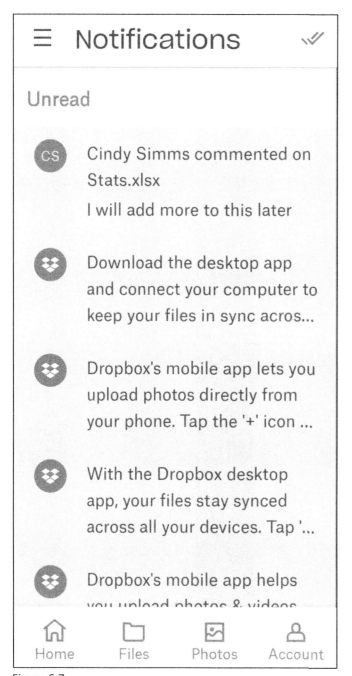

Figure 6.7

Even though the Dropbox app might not be as easy to use as the website on your computer, it's still a handy way to get to your files when you are away from your computer.

Camera Upload

The Dropbox app can be used as a way to back up the photos you have on your smartphone just in case something happens to it such as you lose it, or it gets damaged beyond repair.

Many phones already have a built in backup photo feature such as iCloud for iPhones and Google Photos for Android devices. But if you aren't using one of those services or want to try something different, you can enable the *Camera Upload* feature in the Dropbox app (figure 6.8).

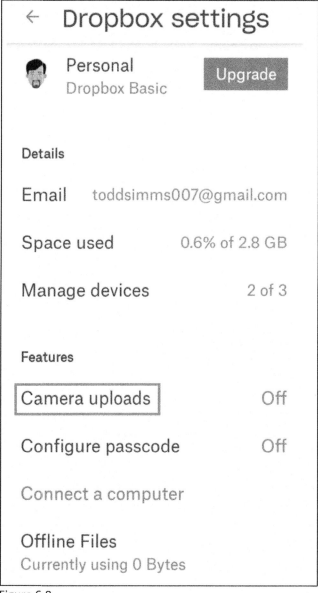

Figure 6.8

To do so, tap on the three horizontal bars in the upper left hand corner and then go to *Settings*. From there, find Camera uploads and turn it on. You can also have the app backup video files to your Dropbox account if you want those copied over as well. Once you have everything configured the way you like, tap on the *Back up my photos* button to start the process.

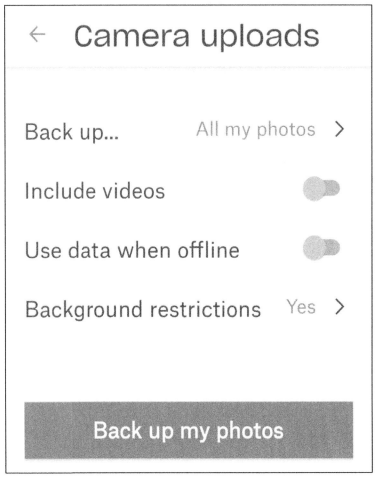

Figure 6.9

 Video files are much larger than image files so if you don't have a lot of space in your Dropbox account then you might find yourself running out of room quickly if you have your smartphone videos backed up along with your photos. This is especially true if you have the Basic free account.

Adding Files and Folders

When it comes to file and folder management, you can add files and folders just like you can with the Dropbox website. To add or create a new file or folder, tap on the blue plus button at the bottom right corner of the app as seen in figure 6.10.

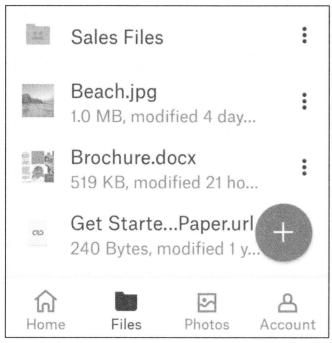

Figure 6.10

Then you will have several options as to what you can add to your account. You can create a new folder or file such as a Word document just like you can on the website. You can also upload existing photos or videos that you have stored on your phone.

The *Take a photo* option will let you take a new picture from your phone and then upload it to your Dropbox account when you are finished. The *Scan document* option will let you use your camera's phone to scan a document into your Dropbox account. Keep in mind that it will not be able to read the text for editing later.

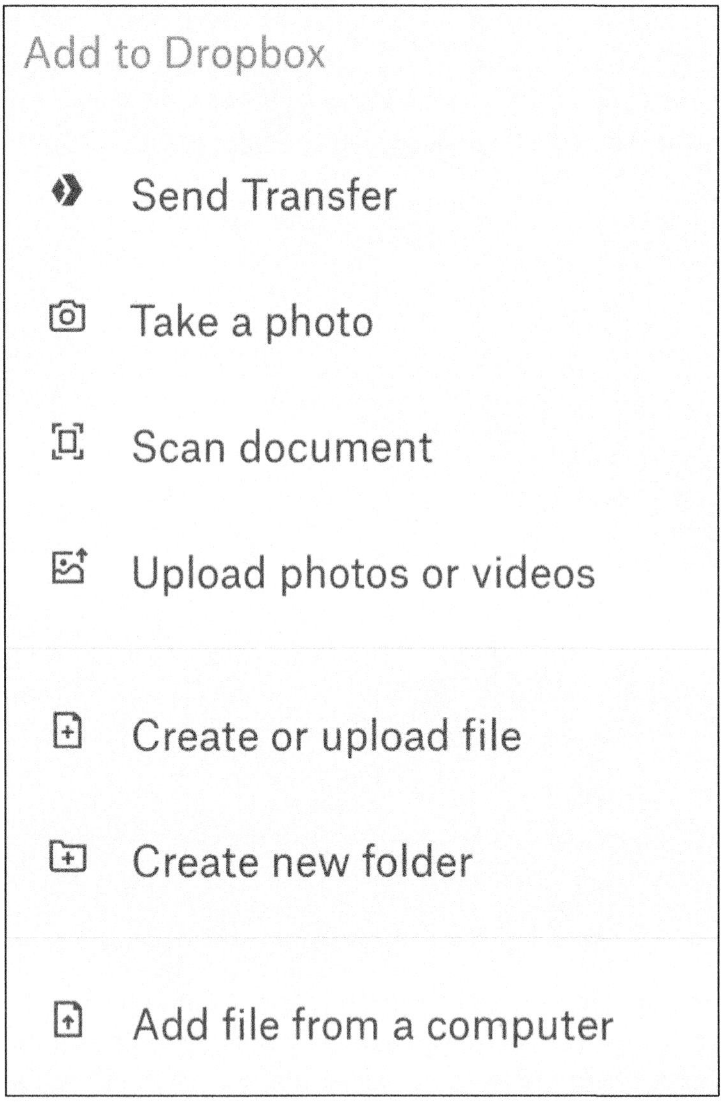

Add to Dropbox

◆❯   Send Transfer

📷   Take a photo

⌞⌝   Scan document

☑   Upload photos or videos

⊞   Create or upload file

⊞   Create new folder

⬆   Add file from a computer

Figure 6.11

If you want to send multiple files to a person, you can use the *Send Transfer* feature to have them packaged up and then have a link created that you can send to the person (figures 6.12 to 6.14).

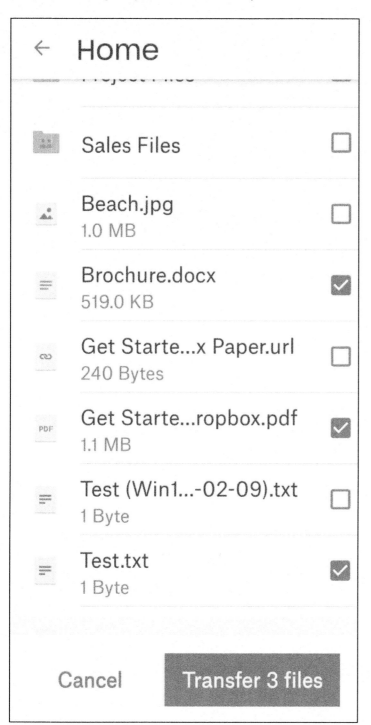

Figure 6.12

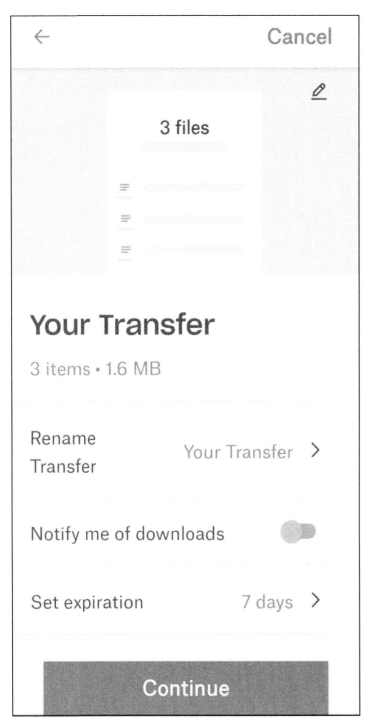

Figure 6.13

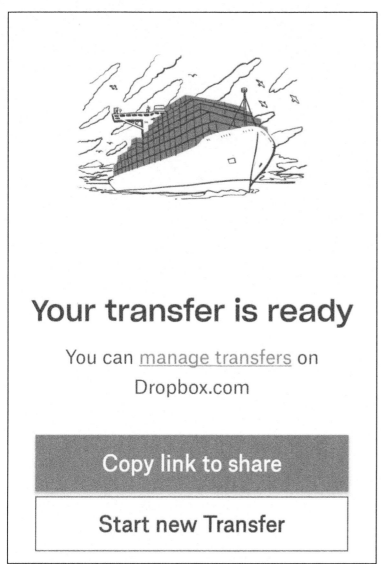

Figure 6.14

Then when they click the link, they will be able to download the files from your transfer (figure 6.15).

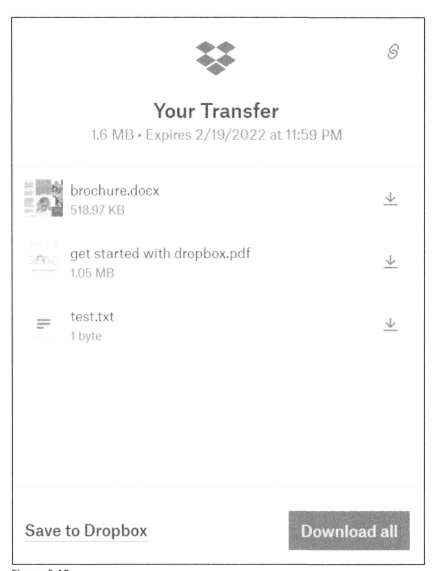

Figure 6.15

Chapter 7 – Advanced Features

Now that I have covered the basics (and then some), you should have a good idea of how to use your Dropbox account and share your files and folders with those who you collaborate with.

As you have been using your Dropbox account, you might have noticed some extra features and might have been wondering what they do and how they work. In this chapter, I will be covering many of these advanced or extra features to help you determine if they are something you would like to take advantage of. Not all of these extra features are available with the free account so I will be sure to let you know what type of account you need to use a feature if that is the case.

Dropbox Scan

In the last chapter on using the Dropbox app on your smartphone, I mentioned how you can use your camera to scan documents into your Dropbox account. Using this method is fairly basic and really only takes a picture of your document and converts it into a PDF or JPG image file.

On the other hand, the Dropbox Scan standalone app is a little more advanced because you can use it to convert physical documents into high quality PDF or PNG files and then send them right to your Dropbox account or share them with others.

It can be used to scan items such as receipts, ID cards, photos and so on so you can have a backup of these important documents. It also supports multi page scanning so you can have a scanned document be more than a single page. You can also adjust your scans when they are complete by adding filters, adjusting the contrast and cropping the scan itself. You can also then share these scans via email, text, instant messenger and so on.

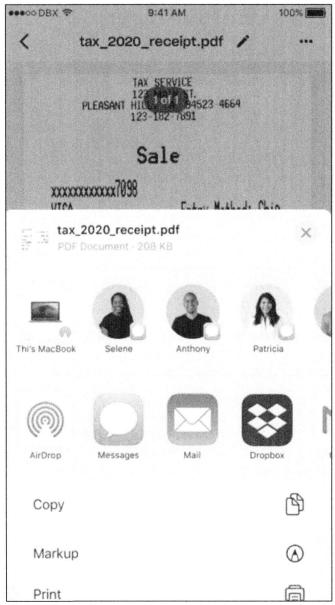

Figure 7.1

As of this writing, the Dropbox Scan app is only available for Apple iPhones and iPads and not for Android devices but hopefully they will have an Android version soon.

Full Text Search

Back in chapter 3, I showed you how to search your files and folders in Dropbox. The basic plan offers... basic searching and if you want to have some more advanced search features, you will need to upgrade to a higher level plan. Actually any plan but the free plan will come with the full text search ability.

The full text search feature will search within documents to find what you are looking for rather than only search the file or folder names. Figure 7.2 shows what happens if I search for **conf room** in the Business plan. As you can see, I get results from folder names, text inside an Excel spreadsheet and also from images.

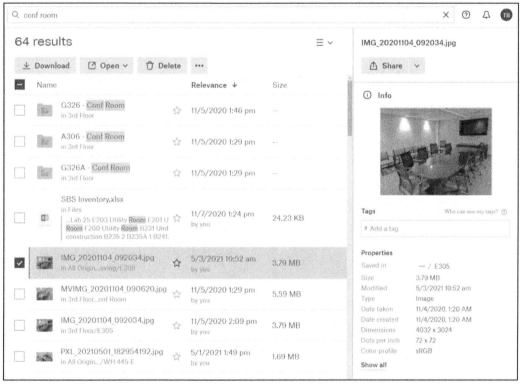

Figure 7.2

There are many types of files that Dropbox can search within but that doesn't mean it will work with every type of file. Below you will find the supported file types listed by their file extension.

- .doc
- .docx
- .docm
- .gdoc
- .gsheet
- .jpg (Dropbox Professional and Business users only)
- .paper

- .papert
- .pdf
- .png (Dropbox Professional and Business users only)
- .ppt
- .pptx
- .pptm
- .gif (Dropbox Professional and Business users only)
- .gslide
- .rtf
- .tiff (Dropbox Professional and Business users only)
- .txt
- .xls
- .xlsx
- .xlsm
- .vtt

Family Room

Dropbox has a feature that is meant to help keep families who might not live close by together by providing a place where they can share files such as photos, recipes, documents and pretty much anything else you would want to share.

The plan gives you 2TB (terabytes) of space to share these files which is actually quite a bit of space. Plus each family member gets their own account that they can use to store their own personal files that will be accessible only to them.

With the Family Plan, you can have up to 6 family members join and participate. The plan also includes additional products and features such as Dropbox Passwords, Dropbox Vault, and computer backup. Dropbox Vault is a PIN protected folder that you can access at any time and on any device and can be used to store documents that need an extra layer of security.

It also comes with the Password app which will let your family create and store account details across their devices such as computers, smartphones and tablets. Plus if your family uses Facebook, they can transfer entire photo and video libraries right into Dropbox without having to download them to their computer first.

The Family Room Plan costs $16.99 per month which isn't a bad price for that many users.

Dropbox Paper

If you have any experience using Google Docs or Microsoft Word Online, then you shouldn't have any problems using Dropbox Paper because it is also an online word processor that you can use for free.

Each one of these platforms has its own benefits so it's up to you as to which one you want to use, or you can also use all three of them. I won't be going over the differences since that would be a whole other book!

If you are working with all Dropbox users, then Paper might be the way to go since everyone will already have an account and won't have to sign up for a Microsoft or Google account. To start a new Paper document, go to the *Create* menu and then choose *Document > Dropbox Paper*.

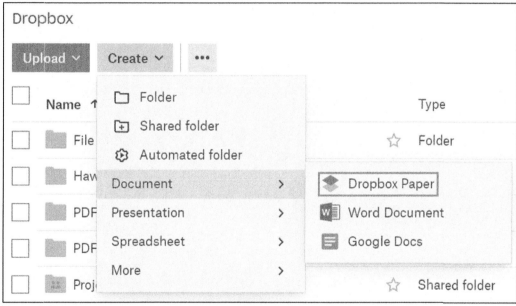

Figure 7.3

When you create a new Paper document, you will be informed that you can share the file just by providing someone with a link and that you can change the settings if you want to prevent them from editing it.

> To share this Dropbox file, just copy the URL from your
> browser. Keep in mind, anyone with the URL may be able to   Change settings   Close
> edit.

Figure 7.4

Clicking on Change settings brings up the familiar share settings box where you can change the permissions from edit to view only.

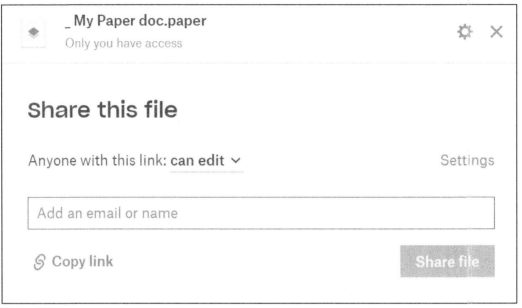

_ My Paper doc.paper
Only you have access

Share this file

Anyone with this link: **can edit** ∨   Settings

Add an email or name

𝒮 Copy link   Share file

Figure 7.5

Dropbox will then present you with a blank Paper document and you can immediately change the name and start adding content.

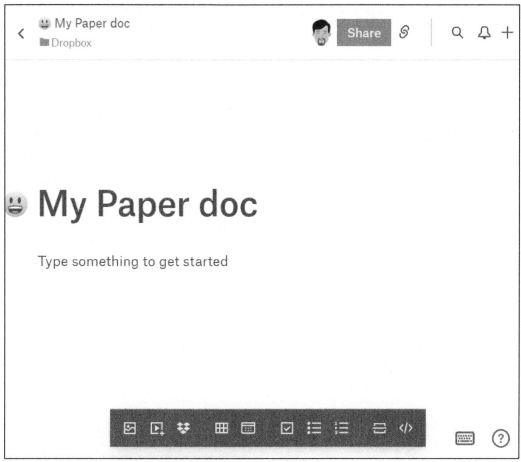

Figure 7.6

You will see a toolbar at the bottom of the page with the editing tools.

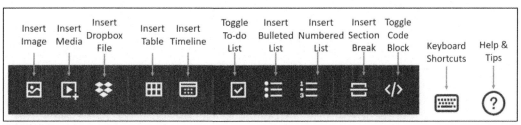

Figure 7.7

As you can see from figure 7.8, it's pretty easy to add some text and an image to create an online document that you can then share with others. But if you share your document with a non Dropbox user, they will need to create an account in order to view it.

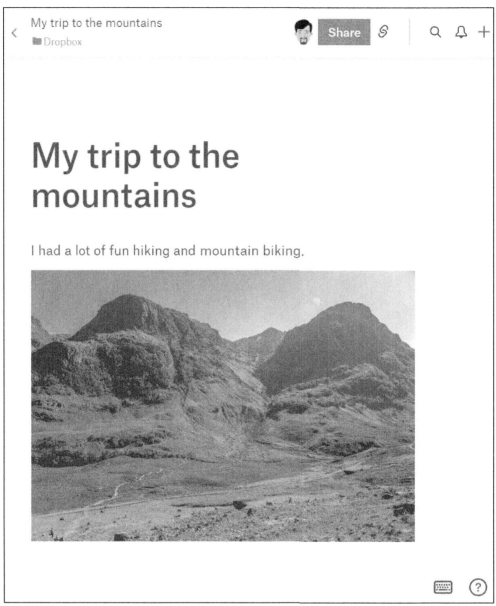

Figure 7.8

After you create your document, you will see it listed with the other files in the folder that you created it in. You can then do things with the file such as move, rename, copy, delete it and so on.

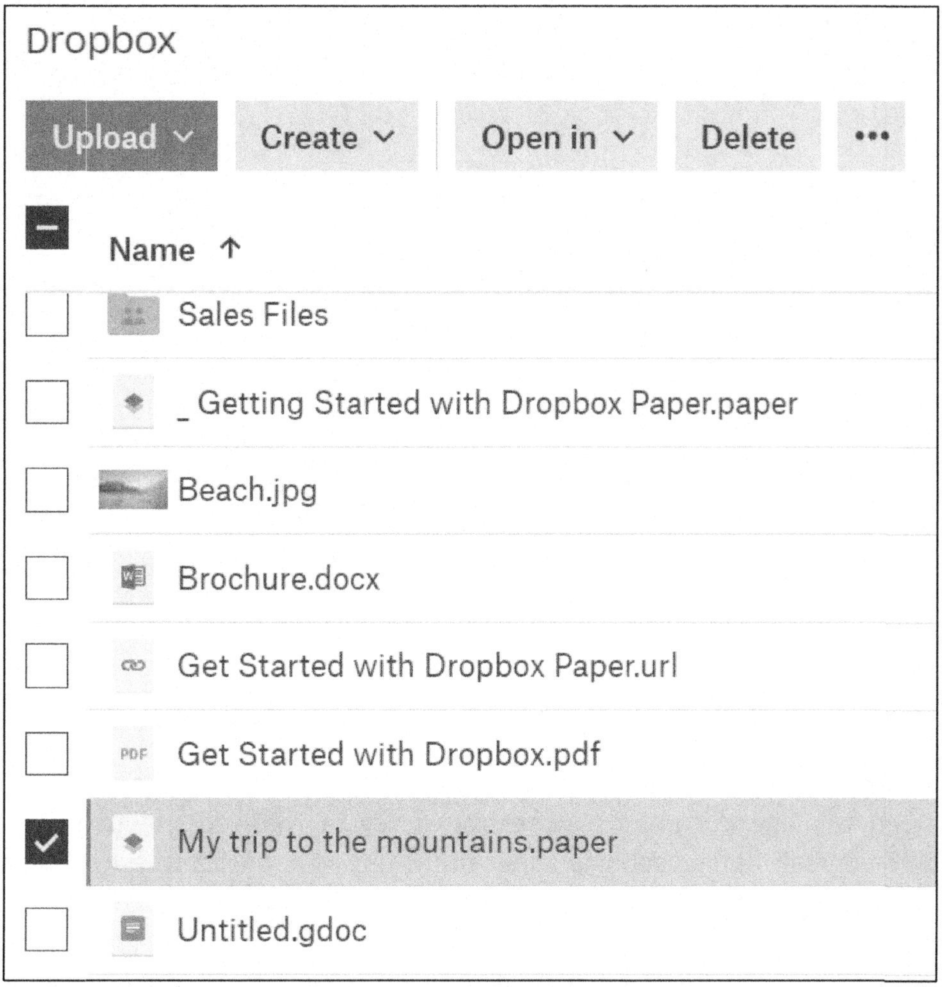

Figure 7.9

One thing to keep in mind when it comes to Dropbox Paper files is that you can't download them to your computer. What you can do though is click on the ellipsis while the file is open and then choose the *Export* option to export the file as a PDF, Word document or Markdown file. I have heard that Dropbox is working on a Paper app that you can install on your computer to open Paper files so keep an eye out for that.

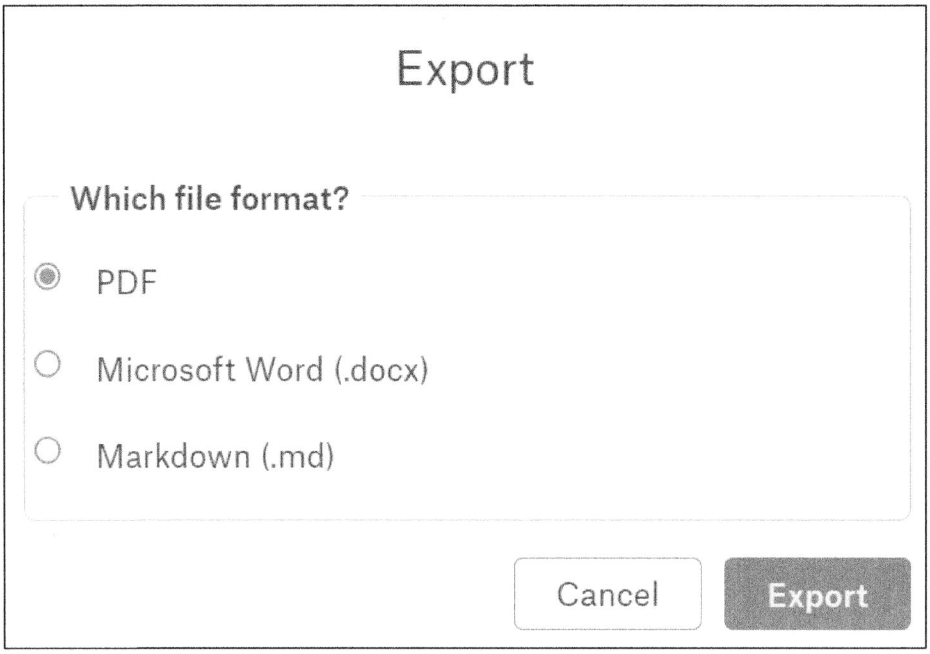

Figure 7.10

HelloSign eSignatures

If you need to have documents signed on a regular basis or need to sign documents yourself before sending them out, then you can use the HelloSign eSignature feature that can be connected to your Dropbox account.

Dropbox includes a limited Free plan where you can make 3 free signature requests per month. But this is only available if you are using a Dropbox Business account.

Once you link your account you can then choose a file from any Dropbox folder to be sent out for a signature.

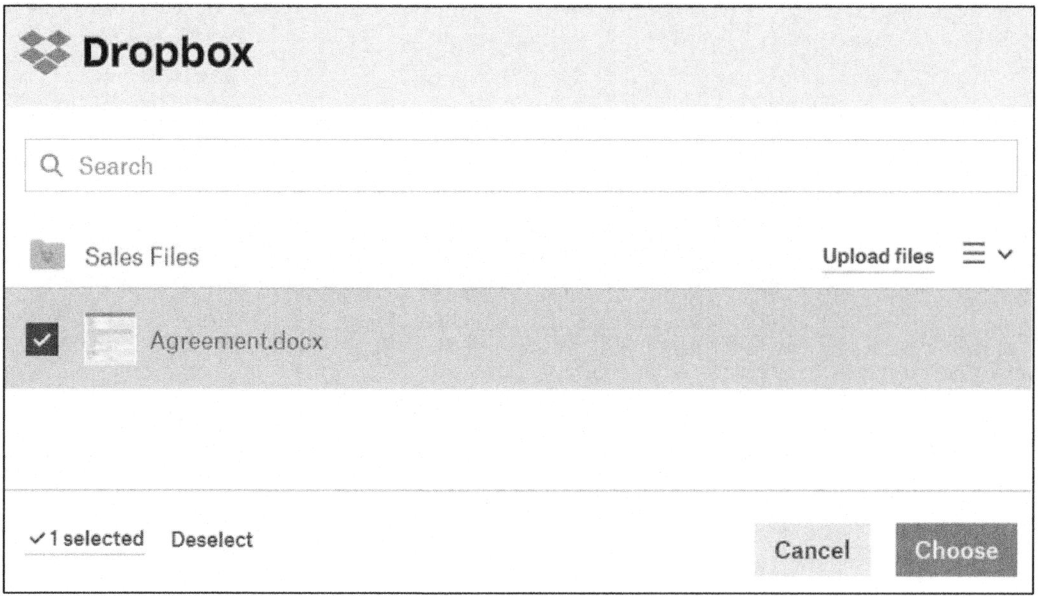

Figure 7.11

Next, you can fill in the names and addresses of the people who need to sign the document.

Figure 7.12

Your document will then be opened in an interface where you can add the signature field along with other fields such as initials, name, date and so on. To add these fields to your document, you can just drag and drop them on the page. You don't need to have preconfigured field boxes like I have in my document.

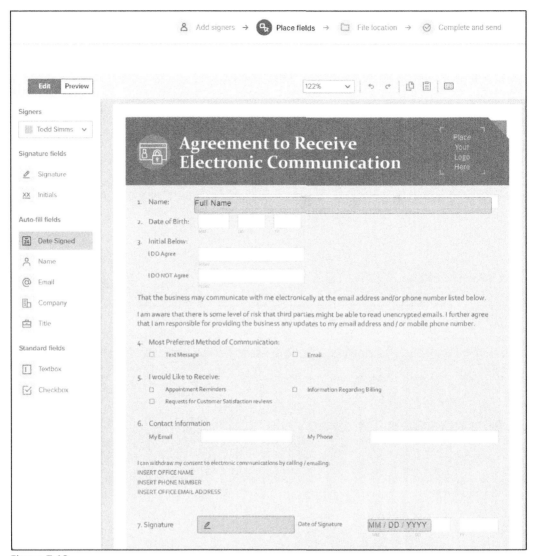

Figure 7.13

Next, you will need to choose the location where the signed document will be stored. You can keep it in the same folder as the original if you like.

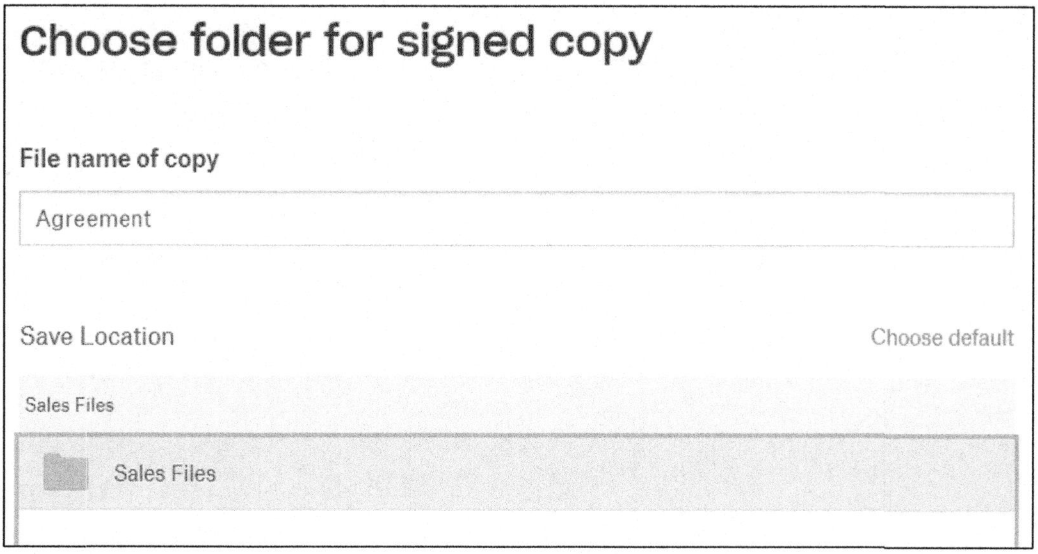

Choose folder for signed copy

File name of copy

Agreement

Save Location   Choose default

Sales Files

📁   Sales Files

Figure 7.14

You can then add an additional message if needed and when everything looks good, you can click on the *Send for signature* button.

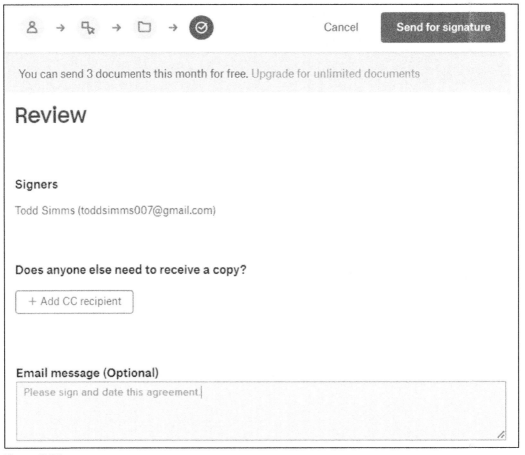

Figure 7.15

Figure 7.16 shows how the email will look when received by the person who needs to sign the document. They can then click on the *Review & Sign* button to start the signing procedure.

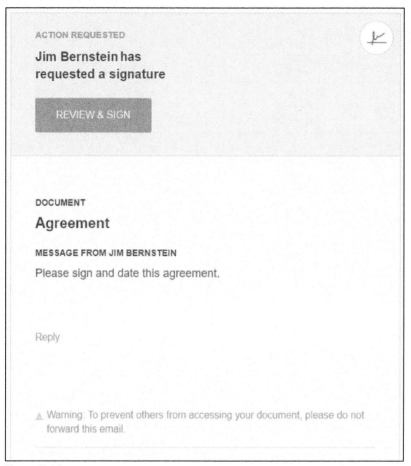

Figure 7.16

If you added a name and date field, they will automatically be filled in based on the name you put in the request and the date the person signs the document. For the signature, they just need to click on the *Click to sign* button to get started.

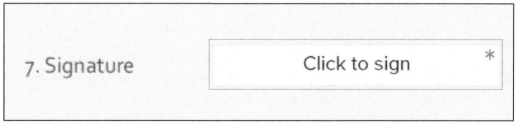

Figure 7.17

They will then have three signing options including signing it with their mouse or finger, typing it in or adding a signature image.

Figure 7.18

Once they click the *Insert* button, their signature will be added to the document.

Figure 7.19

After they sign the document, they can click the *Continue* button and then click on the *I agree* button. Figure 7.20 shows what the email will look like that is sent back to you after they sign it. You can then click on the *View on Dropbox* button to see the signed document, or just go to the folder that you specified the document to be placed in.

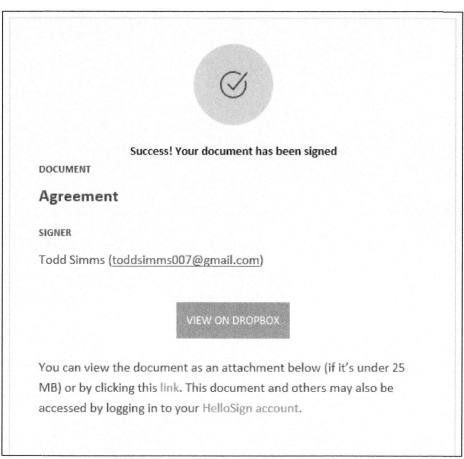

Figure 7.20

You can also check your signature request status page and preview, download or locate the file from there.

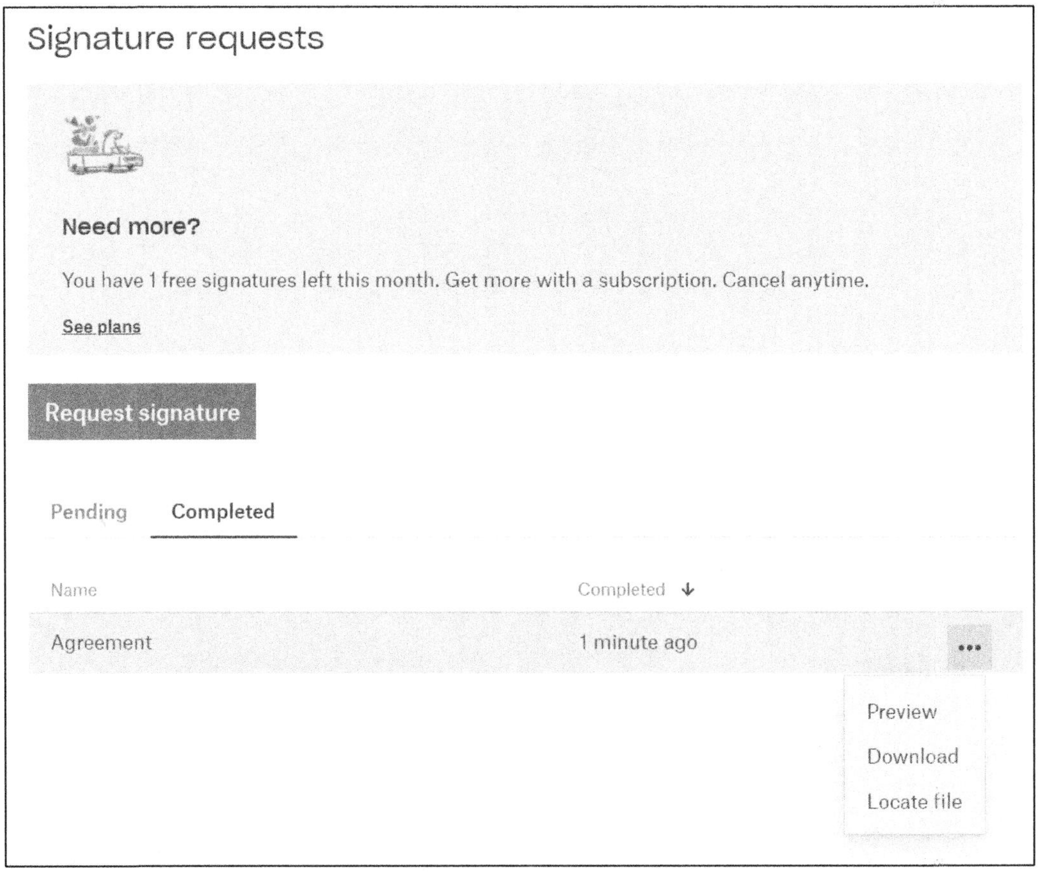

Figure 7.21

At the bottom of the signed document, you will have an audit trail that shows the signature process from start to finish (figure 7.22).

▽ **HELLOSIGN**   Audit Trail

TITLE	Agreement
FILE NAME	Agreement.docx
DOCUMENT ID	c66671610cd7190e11464e257335ab419e45691a
AUDIT TRAIL DATE FORMAT	MM / DD / YYYY
STATUS	● Signed

Document History

↱ SENT	**02 / 14 / 2022** 17:16:04 UTC	Sent for signature to Todd Simms (toddsimms007@gmail.com) from jbernstein IP: 23.240.145.194
◎ VIEWED	**02 / 14 / 2022** 17:23:13 UTC	Viewed by Todd Simms (toddsimms007@gmail.com) IP: 23.240.145.194
↙ SIGNED	**02 / 14 / 2022** 17:26:47 UTC	Signed by Todd Simms (toddsimms007@gmail.com) IP: 23.240.145.194
✓ COMPLETED	**02 / 14 / 2022** 17:26:47 UTC	The document has been completed.

Figure 7.22

Comments

If you are planning to use Dropbox to collaborate with others and share files with the people on your projects, then you might want to take advantage of the comments feature that is available to you in Dropbox.

Using comments is a great way to share your ideas with others on specific files without having to send someone an email etc. When someone opens their Dropbox account, they can see your comment when they look at the file you made your comment on.

To add a comment simply select the file and then from the pop-out pane on the right, go to the Comments section and type one in. If you click on the @ symbol in the comment box, you can direct your comment towards another Dropbox user if they have access to that file as seen in figure 7.23.

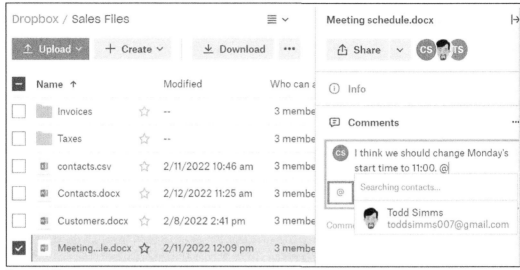

Figure 7.23

Once you type in your comment you can then edit or delete it or add additional comments. You can also reply to a comment that you or someone else has made.

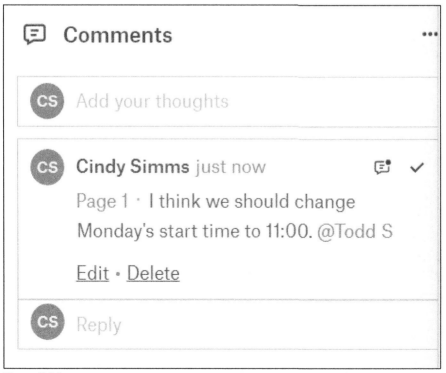

Figure 7.24

Depending on your computer's settings, you might receive a popup notification when someone makes a comment on a file.

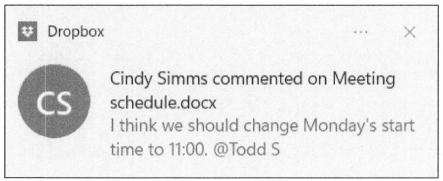

Figure 7.25

Another way to be notified about comments is when you click on a file that has a comment, you will see a notification next to the comment icon.

Figure 7.26

When you open the comments section to view a comment, you can click on the ellipsis and you will have options to show comments that have been resolved, unsubscribe from comments so you don't see them or disable them altogether.

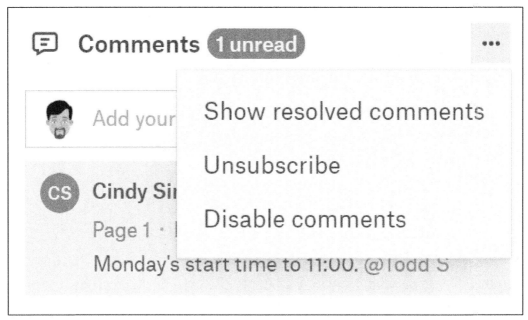

Figure 7.27

You will also get an email notification when someone comments on a file and directs their comment towards you.

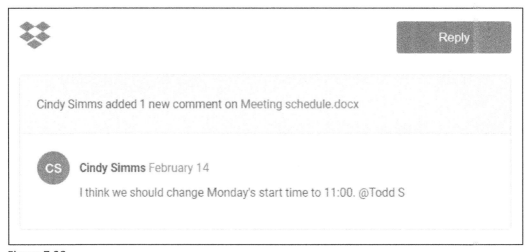

Figure 7.28

Automated Folders

Automated Folders is a newer Dropbox feature and what it does is perform a specific process on any files that are added to that folder such as converting added files to PDF documents etc.

To create an automated folder, click on the *Create* button and choose the *Automated folder* option.

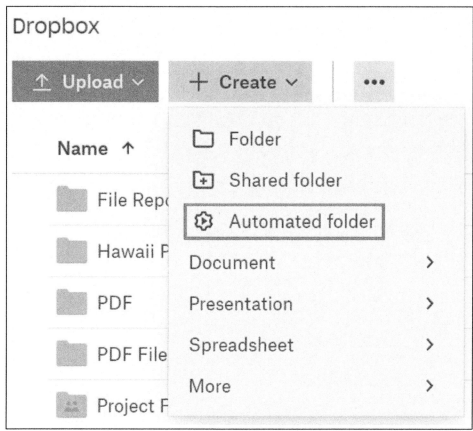

Figure 7.29

Next, you will give the folder a name and choose which type of automation you would like to apply to it (figure 7.30). I will call my folder Meeting Notes and have any files that are added converted to PDF files.

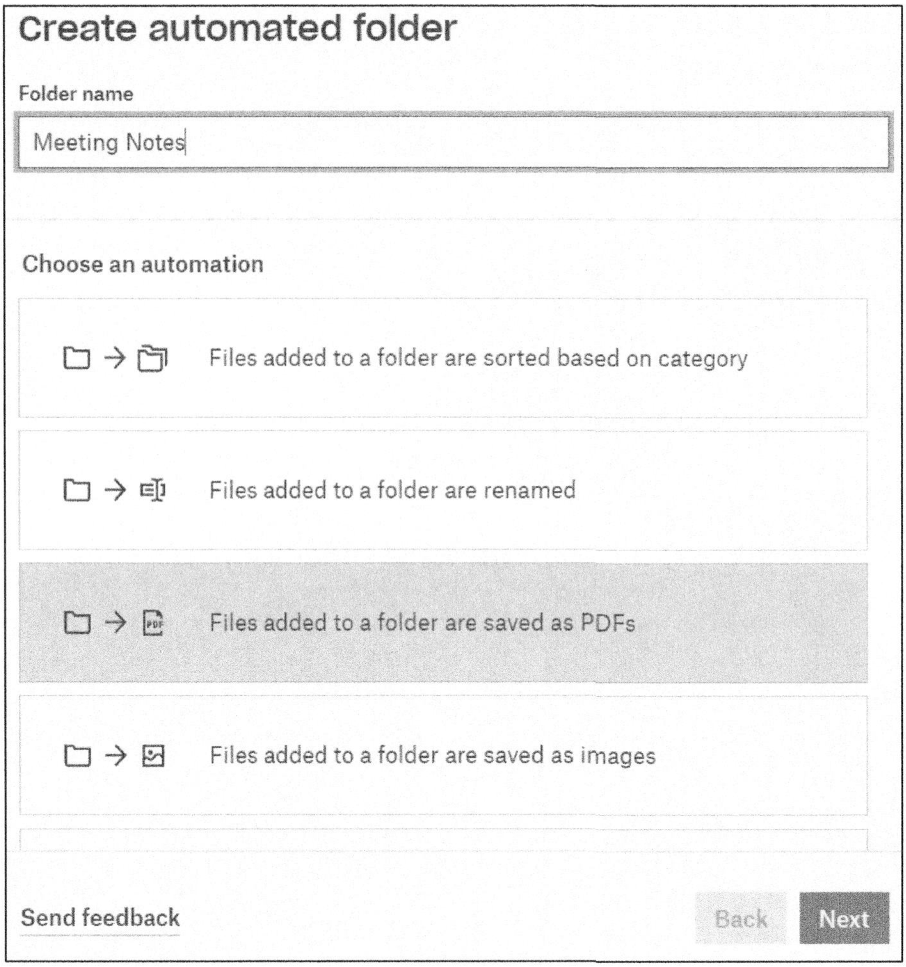

Create automated folder

Folder name

Meeting Notes

Choose an automation

☐ → 🗂   Files added to a folder are sorted based on category

☐ → ▤   Files added to a folder are renamed

☐ → 📄   Files added to a folder are saved as PDFs

☐ → 🖼   Files added to a folder are saved as images

Send feedback   Back   Next

Figure 7.30

For this type of automation, I have the option to choose which types of files I want to apply this process to. I will choose all supported file types. You will have different options depending on what type of automation you choose.

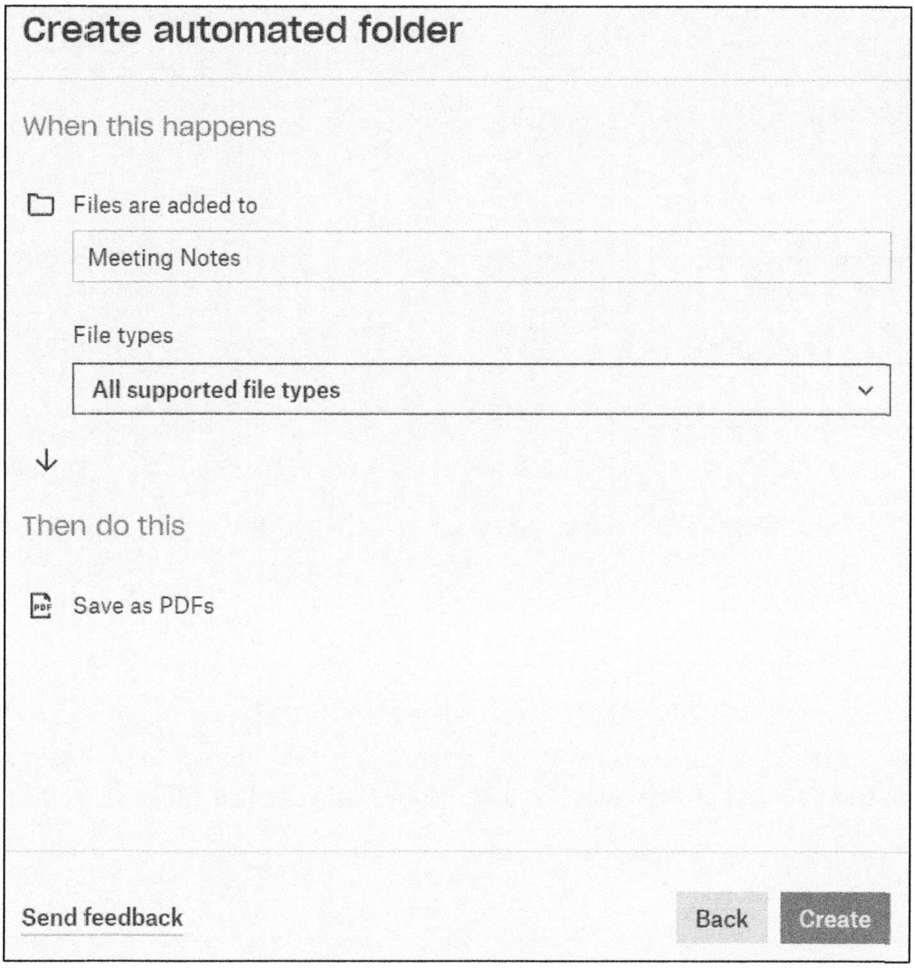

Create automated folder

When this happens

📁 Files are added to

Meeting Notes

File types

All supported file types ⌄

↓

Then do this

📄 Save as PDFs

Send feedback   Back   Create

Figure 7.31

After you create the automated folder, it will be labeled as automated as seen in figure 7.32.

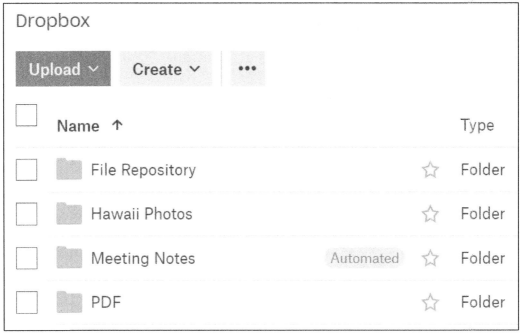

Figure 7.32

Now when I drag some Microsoft Word documents into that folder, I get a notification telling me that they were automatically saved as PDF files.

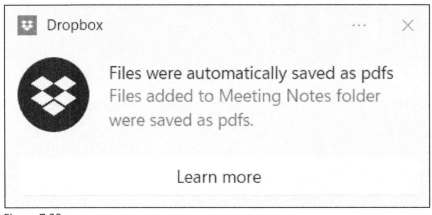

Figure 7.33

When I go to that folder, I will see my original Word files and their associated PDF files.

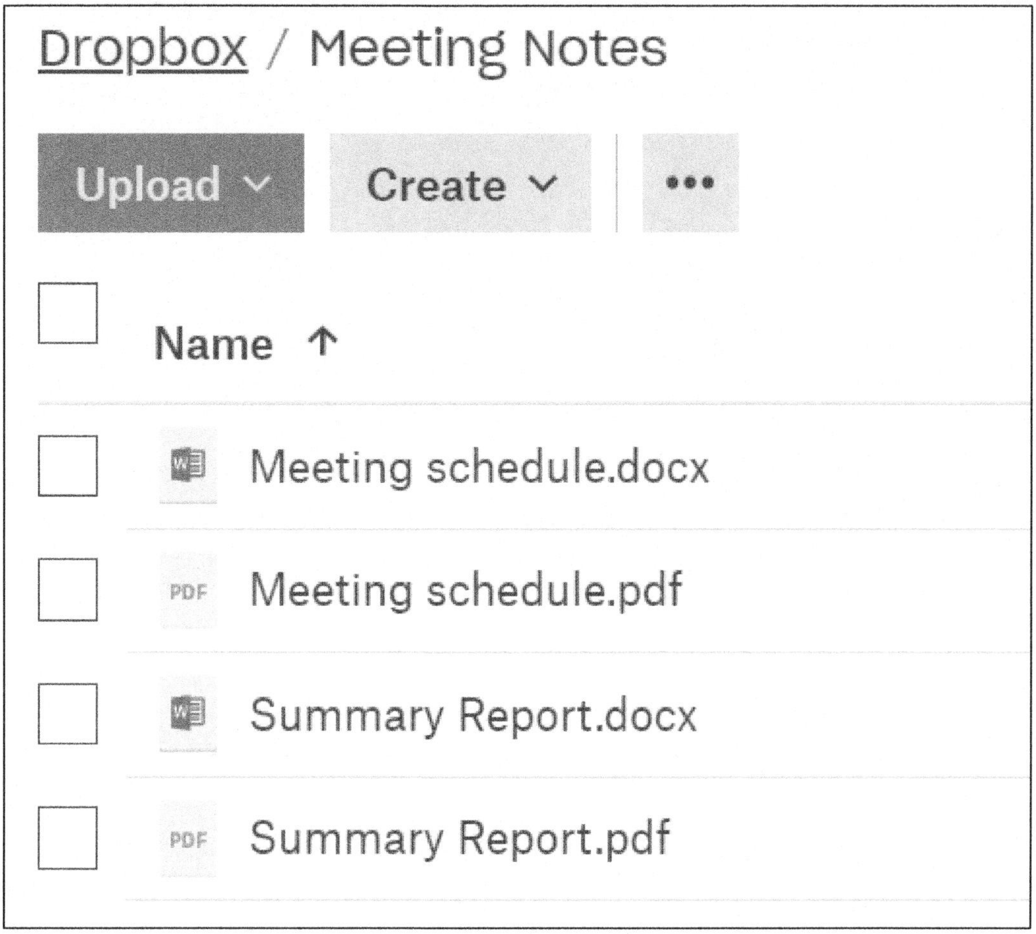

Figure 7.34

Email to Dropbox

If you are the type who finds themselves saving a lot of your email attachments in your DropBox folder then you might want to try the Email to Dropbox feature. What this will do is create a Dropbox email address that you can use to forward any emails to that have attachments that you want to save within your Dropbox account.

To enable the feature, you will need to go to your settings and then find the *Features* section under the *General* category. Once you are there, simply click on *Set up* to get started.

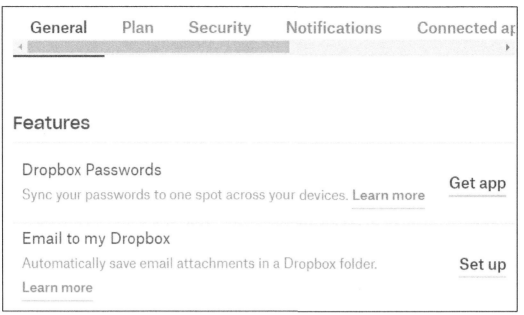

Figure 7.35

You will then be prompted to create a Dropbox email address to be used for this feature. The email address will be created by Dropbox, so you don't have a say in what it actually is.

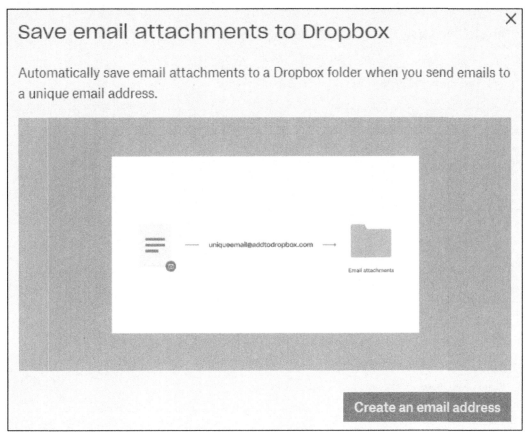

Figure 7.36

Once it creates the email address, you should copy it and save it somewhere such as your email address book, so you don't need to remember it. If someone else gets a hold of this email address, they will be able to forward their own emails to it and have the attachments placed in your account.

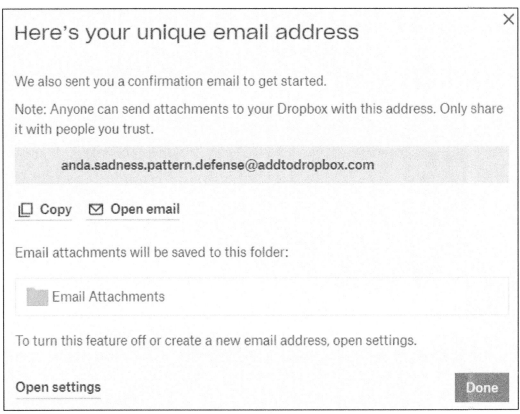

Figure 7.37

Dropbox will also create a folded named *Email Attachments* that will be used to hold all of the attachments that are pulled from the forwarded emails.

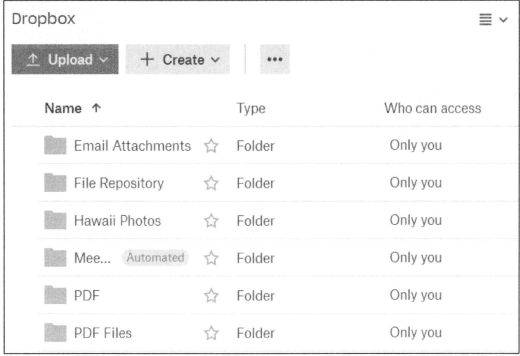

Figure 7.38

If you want to turn the feature off, change the folder or have Dropbox generate a new email address, you can go back to the Features setting and make changes from there.

Personal account

| General | Plan | Security | Notifications | Connected apps | Default ap |

Features

Dropbox Passwords
Sync your passwords to one spot across your devices. Learn more   **Get app**

Email to my Dropbox
Automatically saves email attachments to a folder when
you send emails to   **Get new address** ⓘ   **Turn off**
anda.sadness.pattern.defense@addtodropbox.com

Figure 7.39

Now when you forward an email with an attachment as seen in figure 7.40, the attachment will be uploaded to your Email Attachments folder as seen in figure 7.41.

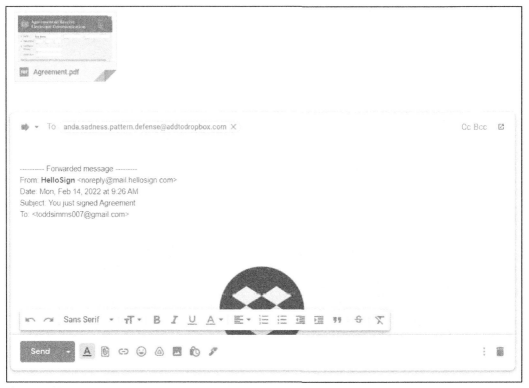

Figure 7.40

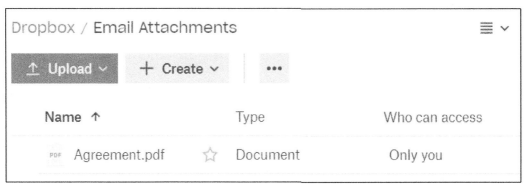

Figure 7.41

What's Next?

Now that you have read through this book and taken your Dropbox skills to the next level, you might be wondering what you should do next. Well, that depends on where you want to go. Are you happy with what you have learned, or do you want to further your knowledge or try out some of the more advanced features that come with the Business, Professional or Advanced plans?

If you do want to expand your knowledge on other cloud technology related topics, you should look at subject-specific books such as cloud storage or hosted servers and services. Focus on one subject at a time, then apply what you have learned to the next subject. You can also check my other books that cover a wider range of topics mentioned above and then some.

There are many great video resources as well, such as Pluralsight or CBT Nuggets, which offer online subscriptions to training videos of every type imaginable. YouTube is also a great source for training videos if you know what to search for.

If you are content in being a Dropbox power user that knows more than your friends, then just keep on reading up on the technologies you want to learn, and you will soon become your friends and family's go-to computer person, which may or may not be something you want!

Thanks for reading **Dropbox Made Easy**. You can also check out the other books in the Made Easy series for additional computer related information and training. You can get more information on my other books on my Computers Made Easy Book Series website.

https://www.madeeasybookseries.com

You should also check out my computer tips website, as well as follow it on Facebook to find more information on all kinds of computer topics.

www.onlinecomputertips.com
https://www.facebook.com/OnlineComputerTips/

About the Author

James Bernstein has been working with various companies in the IT field since 2000, managing technologies such as SAN and NAS storage, VMware, backups, Windows Servers, Active Directory, DNS, DHCP, Networking, Microsoft Office, Exchange, and more.

He has obtained certifications from Microsoft, VMware, CompTIA, ShoreTel, and SNIA, and continues to strive to learn new technologies to further his knowledge on a variety of subjects.

He is also the founder of the website onlinecomputertips.com, which offers its readers valuable information on topics such as Windows, networking, hardware, software, and troubleshooting. Jim writes much of the content himself and adds new content on a regular basis. The site was started in 2005 and is still going strong today

Printed in Great Britain
by Amazon

27854106R00086